MW00986342

I HATE GOD

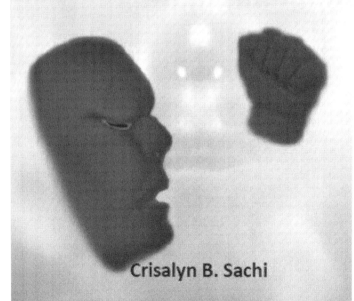

Crisalyn B. Sachi

Copyright © 2015

By Crisalyn B. Sachi

All rights reserved. No part of this book may be reproduced, utilized in or copied in any form-electronic or mechanical-including photocopying, recording or any form of storage or retrieval system, without written permission from the author-Crisalyn B. Sachi. Inquiries should be emailed to crisalynsachi@yahoo.com or go to the website generalmom.com

Scripture quotations are from the Holy Bible, King James Version, KJV. Public Domain

I dedicate this book, 'I Hate God' to do the work of my Heavenly Father. Without His miracles, this book could not have been possible. I love You God and I give You the glory. Happy Father's Day to the Father of all fathers.

I also dedicate this book to my biological father, James Millard Jones. Thank you Dad for sharing your part of this testimony because without it, 'I Hate God' would not be complete. I released this book in the month of June to honor you for your birthday, which was on May 24, 2015 and for Father's Day. Happy Birthday and Happy Father's Day. I love you Dad.

Love Your Daughter,
Crisalyn B. Sachi

Acknowledgements

I would like to thank everyone who made this book possible. First, I thank God who orchestrated some amazing miracles to make this book come alive and to prove His existence. I would like to thank my editors Brenda Stone Browder, Minister Michelle Daniels, BA and MATLT, Bonnie Davis, Vida Williams, and my aunt, Rachel Mitchell. I thank my evaluators Robert Michael Carreker, Keith Brandon, Pamala Jones-Braddy, my step-daughter, Kennya Slaughter, and Minister Janet Davis for reviewing this project. I give a special mention to my father, James Millard Jones, my son, Robertrel A. Sachi, and my daughter, Thiessalyn S. Sachi who helped me with some of my technical issues and the stories that were a part of this book. I would also like to thank, my uncle, Dale Mitchell for the use of his name in this true story. All of our stories together, gave 'I Hate God' a personal touch. I give God the glory for everything.

The true accounts that are in this memoir is to help anyone in need of a life changing transformation. Through a father and daughter's experiences, this mind-boggling story 'I Hate God' is written to stimulate your thought process of your self-evaluation. The intent is to stir up your spirit and lead you to a decision based on that outcome. The two lives in 'I Hate God' were very transparent as they poured out their life's stories. One of them verbalized that they hated God while the other one hated God through their lifestyle. This book also addresses some of the current issues and concerns of our nation and our lives.

Do you hate God? God is giving us every opportunity to serve Him. He will reward us with a life of eternity in the kingdom of Heaven. You can serve the Lord with your freewill. The choice is up to you.

TABLE OF CONTENTS

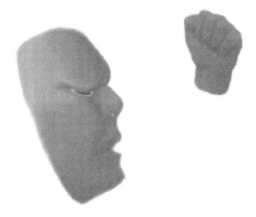

WHO'S MY DADDY

The snowstorm was fierce on a Saturday afternoon while the icy cold winds were gushing snow everywhere. At the same time, the house was warm, heartfelt, and comfortable while my great-grandmother prepared dinner. She was an exceptional cook. The aroma filled the house with the smell of fried chicken. This was my mother's maternal grandmother and I loved her dearly.

I can recall different memories since the age of two. My grandparents had their youngest child late in life. My uncle was nine years old and I was merely five. His name was Dale. We were playing games upstairs not knowing the pain, which was about to follow.

My grandfather was the only dad I knew. No one told me otherwise and I did not know anything different.

I just happened to gaze outside as my grandparents were arriving for the family gathering. My uncle was confused and angry because he did not understand or liked the fact that I was calling his father, Dad. He could not make any sense out of this chaos. After all, we were living a lie. When Dale exposed the truth that day, my life changed its course.

I excitedly yelled as I pointed out the window, "Look, there's Dad and Grandma."

Dale rudely interrupted with anger, "Crissy, I am sick and tired of you calling my dad, Dad. He is not your dad; the truth is; he is your grandfather."

Puzzled in the state of astonishment, I asked, "Why would you say that Dale? He is my dad, just like he is your dad."

"No, he isn't." He replied sternly, "He is your grandfather and you need to stop calling him Dad."

I was in denial. I did not want to believe what I was hearing.

Dale's knowledge was credible. He began to ask me a series of questions. In a sarcastic tone he asked, "Okay then, why do you call his wife Grandma, but your mother and I call him Dad and we call his wife Mom?"

I was not a stupid child. Reality began to sink in and I proceeded to go into shock.

Hysterically, I stuttered, "No… no… no."

That was all I could say repeatedly while my uncle was talking. He could no longer bear the lies. He did not understand this set up any more than I could. The only difference was; he was old enough to see through what I could not see.

As the truth began to unfold before my face, he continued firmly, "You call your mother Mom and I am your uncle. Your mother is my sister, but I am not your brother. If we had the same dad, wouldn't you be my sister too?"

I was in such shock at this point; I just started to scream at the top of my lungs. I could not speak or cry. I was too hurt and crushed. The truth slapped me hard, but not as much as it was getting ready to beat me down to the ground. The anguish was more than I could endure.

My mother ran upstairs first. My grandparents and my great-grandmother followed her. My mother grabbed me to comfort me because she had never heard me scream like this.

My mother said with deep concern, "Crissy, what's wrong?"

I kept screaming and I could not answer.

She desperately insisted, "Crissy, are you listening? Dale, what did you do to her?" She looked at him as though she demanded an answer.

Shamelessly, Dale replied, "I did not do anything to her. I just told her the truth that our dad is not her dad."

When I think about it, my uncle did not have anything to be ashamed about because the truth needed to come out sometime. We all were living a lie and it needed to end. It was abrupt and unexpected, but it was necessary for all parties involved, especially me.

My mother's confirmation made me faint.

With anger, my mother said, "Why did you have to tell her that Dale?"

Since she did not say it was not true, I was out like a light. When I came to, my grandfather was beside me rubbing my arm as I was lying in the bed. He looked just as wounded as I was. My mother, grandmother, and great-grandmother kept getting him cold washcloths to put on my head. My grandfather continued to comfort me.

With his soothing voice my grandfather whispered, "Crissy, don't worry, I will always be your daddy. You can call me Dad as long as you like."

Even though he told me I could call him Dad, it was not the same. I knew now he was not my real father. This was a very painful day in my life, but it was also liberating. The Bible says:

"And ye shall know the truth, and the truth shall make you free."
John 8:32 KJV

It was a hard pill to swallow, but I was free from a malicious lie. This falsehood never should have started in the first place. This man was indeed my grandfather. I did however; call him Dad until my mother remarried. I began my quest to find myself a father. At this age, I did not know I could not pick my own parent. This activated my search for a dad; however, the emptiness for my own biological father grew stronger with a serious hunger in my spirit.

When my mother went to the bank one day, there was a very tall and handsome man in front of her. My mother never let me live this story down and I still remember it to this day.

Desperate for a father, I said, "Mama, tell he who your name is so he can marry you and be my daddy."

(Laugh out loud.) Remember I was only five years old. Those were my exact words. My mother, of course, was embarrassed. She did not say anything to the person. The man just turned around and smiled at both of us.

When we got out of the bank, in the midst of my

mother's humiliation, she said, "Crissy, don't you ever say anything like that again to anyone. Do you hear me?"

With my head hung down, I responded, "Yes, ma'am."

By the time I was seven years old, my mother remarried. I did not accept this man at first. Actually, I cried and begged my mother not to marry him during the ceremony.

Frantically I sobbed, "Mama, please don't marry him. I do not want him to be my daddy. Please don't do it Mama."

My sister on the other hand, excitedly asked, "Can I call him daddy yet?"

She was four years old. She repeated their wedding vows and kept asking the same question between each line.

I cried through the entire ceremony. No matter how much I begged and pleaded with them not to get married, they both still smiled and continued with the marriage.

After four or five months, this man grew on me. I began to realize that he was not going to harm me. I began to call him Dad. I loved him as a daughter would love a father. Because I knew, I had a biological father, my heart still desired to know whom my true father was. He was the other half of my personality. I did not understand part of my character. I needed to know, "Who was Crisalyn?" My biological father was a missing piece of my life who held the mysterious answers, which were unknown to me.

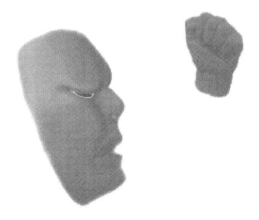

THE JET MAGAZINE

I was in the fifth grade and I was a typical little girl. As I think about it, I had many talents as a small child. I could knit, crochet, embroidery, and make potholders. Furthermore, I could draw, paint, sew by hand or with the sewing machine, and play the piano. I was always finding something to do to keep busy. I made good grades. I enjoyed learning new things and I really loved school.

One day, my mother was waiting on me to come home from school. It was the end of spring in 1967. School was almost out for the summer. I was wondering if I was in trouble for something, by the way she looked at me. The terrible news that she had to tell me, I would have rather been in trouble because it would have been a better outcome.

Reluctantly, my mother gestured, "Come here and sit down Crissy. We need to talk."

I uneasily responded, "Yes, ma'am. What's wrong?"
Hesitantly my mother handed me a publication and replied, "Well, I will let you read it."
With a bewildered face, I said, "Okay."
My mother gave me the 'Jet Magazine.' She opened it to the page she wanted me to read. As I began to read, my heart dropped. The article was about my father, James Millard Jones. He robbed a bank in Urbana, Iowa. He had a gun, and apparently, he kidnapped a woman. He wore a black mask and no one could identify him. In court, the woman could only recognize his voice. The 'Jet' said that my father received ten years for robbing the bank and ten years for having a weapon. The rest of the ninety-nine years was for holding a woman, as a hostage against her will and taking her to Waterloo, Iowa. The authorities and the court system had gotten my father on circumstantial evidence. I was ready to cry, but I could not for some reason.
My mother wanted to make sure I was fully aware of what I read. She questioned me sternly, "You do know who this is, don't you?"
Astounded and hurt, I replied, "Yes, ma'am."
"I told you," As she, argued arrogantly, "you are better off without your father."
Of course, I did not look at it the way she did. I still wanted to meet my father. I did not understand why she did not comprehend my need. She knew her father all of her life. She knew who she was. I had an emptiness. Yes, my father who raised me was a marvelous man, but my DNA was screaming for my biological father. He was the missing link that I needed to explain my character.
Seeing this in the magazine, took hope away from

me. I began to wonder if I would ever see my father. When I went to bed that night, I cried myself to sleep.

From this point of my life, I prayed, "God, please let me see my father one day. I still love him even though I don't know him."

God heard a child's prayer. God comforted my aching heart. I knew as a child, my father would out-live my parents. I do not know how I knew this, but I did. Unfortunately, this is what happened.

Years later, my father told me how his dad came to see him in the prison in Cedar Rapids, Iowa. He flew from Pittsburg, Pennsylvania. The prison allowed my father a little bit of time to see his dad. Escorted by the guards, my father could see my grandfather was scared and concerned.

My father greeted his dad disgracefully. With an apprehensive look on his father's face, my grandfather sighed, "You done did it now Son."

Looking at his father regretfully, my father replied, "I know Dad."

With an arrogant attitude, his father asked, "Do you know who has you now Son?"

My father was bewildered with his dad's behavior and his question. He reluctantly responded, "No, sir."

My grandfather answered his son harshly, "The United States of America."

My father never looked at it from this perspective. Reality sunk in; now, he was concerned. My grandfather reminded him that the documents stated, 'The United States of America verses James Millard Jones.'

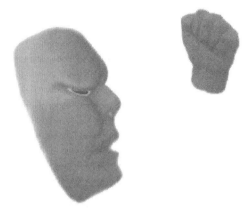

THE LETTER

As James Millard Jones sat in his prison cell, and thought about his life, the angrier he became. He hated everything about himself and his heart was full of rage. He lost his first wife, daughter, and his freedom. He took the blame for losing his freedom and maybe even his wife, but my father refused to take the blame for losing his only child. I was born as Crisalyn Jones. I became a Smith after my adoption in the third grade. Yes, James Millard Jones is my biological father. In his mind, there was nothing in the world he could have done so bad to have lost his precious daughter. He had only seen me once in his entire life when I was two.

Many people judged him. Who are they to judge him when they had a life full of sin? He knew he was not perfect, but neither were they. The Bible says:

"Judge not, that ye be not judged.

For with what judgement ye judge, ye shall be judged: and with what measure ye mete, it shall be measured to you again."
Matthew 7:1-2 KJV

Furthermore, it says:

"So when they continued asking him, he lifted up himself, and said unto them, He that is without sin among you, let him first cast a stone at her."
John 8:7 KJV

My father was even angry at the only perfect Being whom created us all. He blamed God for taking his daughter from him. He hated every person on this earth and he hated God. Yes, he hated God. He had no problems verbalizing it to anyone who would listen. This was his state of mind and no one could tell him anything different. It was my father against the world and God. To make matters worse, he was falling deeper into a world of darkness, which would take him years to convert into a man who could actually love someone.

As animosity and fury consumed my father's spirit in March of 1975, he remembered what a beautiful day it was. He decided to write God a very bitter letter. He had no idea of who God really was. It says in the Word of God:

"And God said unto Moses, I AM THAT I AM: and he said, Thus shalt thou say unto the children of Israel, I AM hath sent me unto you."
Exodus 3:14 KJV

My father figured since he was going to go to Hell anyway, he was going to take many other people with him. He knew that one day he would just meet them there because of their evil ways. My father put a lot of profanity in the letter as he poured his hateful heart out to God. Yeah, he was bold enough to cuss out God. Just like some people, I was surprised that God did not strike him down dead on the spot. By the time, you finish reading this book; you will know how powerful, merciful, loving, and forgiving God is. My father's letter went something like this:

Dear God,
    You have really made me mad. You have let people steal my daughter from me. I know that I have not been a saint, but I have not done anything so evil to lose my only child. I know that I have hurt many people, but if this is Your way of punishing me, don't You think that my being in prison is enough? What kind of God are You to let me suffer by letting my only child grow up without me? Yes, I am talking to You God. I hate what You have done to me and I hate You God. I know my daughter's mother is teaching her to hate me. This makes us all even because I hate everyone too. If You are real God like You say You are, You will make my daughter come find and visit me. If she does not come, then You don't exist and You are not God. However, if You are God, I will be seeing my daughter soon.

James Millard Jones

What can I say? This was how he felt, so he wrote God this letter. Take notice in the letter that it said God would make me come find and visit him. I want you to remember this significant point. My father went to the courtyard. He folded and put the letter in a tree. He did this in the late part of the afternoon. He could not explain the deepest feelings of the hatred and rage consuming his heart. You know it had to be intense when he truly believed he was going to Hell, yet it did not stop him from writing the letter. The bad part about it is; he did not care if he went to the Lake of Fire. He would joke about it to the other prisoners.

My father would tell them, "I know that I am going to Hell, and I know I will be seeing you there with me."

The Bible says:

"But the fearful, and unbelieving, and the abominable, and murderers, and whoremongers, and sorcerers, and idolaters, and all liars, shall have their part in the lake which burneth with fire and brimstone: which is the second death."
Revelation 21:8 KJV

My father knew about Heaven and Hell. Whenever he made jokes about this, all of them would laugh and they would tell my father how crazy he was. They really did not know him because he was limited to what he could do behind bars. This man was tough and he held his own.

After my father ate his dinner, the weather began to change. He went to his cell. The sky was dark and the winds were picking up its speed. At first, my father did not think anything about it. As time went by, the weather became violent. The winds were howling with a strong force. About seven o'clock or so, the sirens began to sound. For the first time in his adult life, he was petrified. My father knew he had angered God with the letter he wrote. He stayed in his cell. He wondered, "What have I done?"

My father knew he was going to die this night. He knew he was going to meet his Maker. He knew God was furious. He regretted writing God the letter. He did not want to think about it so my father went to sleep. He did not expect to see the next day. He figured that if he was going to die, he was not going to be awake to see the death angel. My father knew he was going straight to Hell that night.

The next morning, all was calm outside. It was about sixty-five degrees. More importantly, my father was not dead. He was shocked to be among the living. Why did God spare him? My father knew that he surely did not deserve to live. Did he change his evil ways and heart after the Lord gave him another chance? No, my father still hated God.

I would describe my father as being curious and terrified at the same time. He just knew the letter he wrote, was not in the tree. After all of the chaos from the weather the previous night, why would it be? How could it be there with all the raging winds, lightening, and rain? It was impossible. After all, my father really did not expect to get an answer back from God. He just went through the motions. He wanted to vent and tell God, how he felt. It took guts, but my father did it.

It was time to go to breakfast. This is where my father found out that a tornado had ripped through Atlanta. My father was stunned and speechless. There was one thing he was definitely certain of, the letter he wrote would not be in the tree. If a tornado hit, for sure this letter was history. After my father ate, he went to the courtyard to the tree. Some of the limbs were missing and the courtyard had debris everywhere. The letter was still right where he put it. My father was scared to death when he looked across the street. The tornado leveled a store and some of the houses to the ground.

He could not get the letter right away because he was trembling in his shoes. My father had the fearlessness to write God this letter, but he did not have the nerve to get it out of the tree. After pulling himself together, he reached for the letter. He noticed that all of the words he wrote were no longer on the paper. The black ink had disappeared and only the light green and red lines on the paper were still in their place. None of the lines on the paper bled from being in the rain. The paper looked freshly torn from the tablet. He stood there in disbelief. No words can explain my father's feelings as he stared at the empty letter. Since the words on the paper vanished, my father only stood there in shock. Nobody can explain this supernatural event. God is almighty and has divine powers. Instead of my father submitting, he became more violent with God as he stared at the damaged surroundings.

He did not understand and was not going to try. His heart was too deep into hatred to let what happened concerning this letter and the tornado sink into his mind. He had just witnessed one of God's amazing miracles without knowing it. Instead, his rage and hatred increased. My father became furious with God for not allowing him a chance to escape prison. Dad balled up the letter and threw it in the trash. It was many years later when he finally articulated these events regarding this letter. As soon as he told me, I recognized this was truly a miracle from the Most High.

God is so amazing. Forty years ago from March 2015, my father put a letter in a tree to God. On the fortieth anniversary of this event, God gave me the title and the vision for this book. He told me to write the true accounts, which happened concerning my father and me. His divine timing and orchestration never ceases to amaze me. I would have never in a million years; believe that I would be the author of a book called 'I Hate God.' I give all of the glory to God for allowing me to serve Him and to do His will.

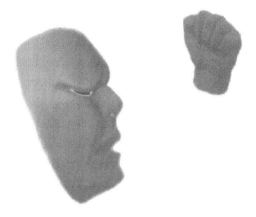

UNCONTROLLABLE BODY

It was a beautiful summer day in July of 1975. I was at Ohio State in Columbus, Ohio. I went to summer school this particular year. Many unexplainable events happened to me during this time. I personally thought I was going insane. I was only nineteen years old. I can say this much, I was truly frightened and I did not understand what was going on with me. Today, I can honestly say, God gets all of the glory for all of these factual experiences in this chapter.

After leaving my morning class, I went back to my room and my roommates were gone. I began to study one of my subjects. All of the lights were on, so it was very bright in the room. All of a sudden, I could not see and everything was pitch black. I thought I had gone blind. I was petrified.

Terrified as I sat in my chair, I thought, "I can't see. What is wrong with me? What's going on?"

I began to see something in front of me. I saw tan square prison bars and I felt like I was floating. As I glided through the corridor, the bars opened for me. When I passed by the first set of bars, I could hear them slamming behind me with a big boom. I floated up to the second set of bars and they opened. Again, the bars slammed behind me with a loud noise. I floated until I appeared in front of a jail cell. I saw a man sitting on the floor next to a painting. I could not make out who the man was or what he looked like. He held his head down with his arms resting on his knees. However, I could make out the painting. It was a painting of a very angry detestable cowboy. You could feel his extreme hateful mannerism in his face. He looked as though he could kill somebody. Looking at this painting, gave me the chills. As fast as I became blind, I suddenly regained my sight.

Needless-to-say, I could not concentrate on my studies for the rest of the day. Instead, I took a walk around campus. Since it was so beautiful outside, I walked to the Oval. This place was in the center of campus. Many students went there to study while they sat on the grass. Some of the students played games or walked their dogs. I went there to rethink what had just happened to me. I was trying to analyze my experience of going blind and viewing the prison image. I had never seen tan prison bars in person or on television. They were always black. I was wondering, "Why were the bars tan?"

I could not get this vision out of my head. It disturbed me. I was not close enough to God to understand that He was trying to tell me something. I did not know that I had just seen a vision. I did figure out that since my father was in prison, this image had something to do with him. I would have rather postponed finding my father until after I graduated college: however, I could not put this experience behind me.

A few days later, I was standing in my bedroom getting ready to go to class. For a second time, I became completely blind. The vision repeated itself and I thought to myself, "Oh no, not again."

I saw every tan prison doors open and close with a loud sound. The man was still sitting on the floor near the hateful cowboy painting. I could not move because I was afraid of falling. I found this experience to be upsetting. I did not want to see these images and most of all; I did not want to be blind. Just as quickly I became blind, I immediately could see.

This time, I had to find out what to do so I called my mother because she was a Christian. However, she was not knowledgeable in this area emotionally or spiritually. She did not know how to explain my circumstances. She could not recognize these visions were coming from God. She doubted my entire story and me.

When my mother answered the phone, she was unaware something was wrong. She had an exuberant response, "Hey Crissy, how is school?"

Unenthusiastically I began to explain, "Well, that is why I am calling you. I have gone blind twice."

Shocked and concerned she asked, "What do you mean you have gone blind twice?"

I did not want my mother to think I was crazy. I was also scared something medically was wrong with me. I had to tell my mother the truth and all of my concerns.

With much reservation, I clarified, "Mom, a few days ago and today, I was studying in my room. I had the lights on in my room and over my desk. All of a sudden, it was pitch black. Mom, I abruptly became blind."

Confused my mother interrupted, "Crissy, that doesn't make any sense. Are you sure you weren't dreaming?"

Trying to convince her, I insisted, "Mom, I was studying. I never went to sleep. I was awake the whole time and wait, there is more to tell you."

I continued to tell my mother, my story. She was surprised these occurrences happened twice. She did not know what to believe.

Sounding doubtful, she said, "So why do you think you saw these things?"

Knowing in my heart that my mother did not want to talk about my father, I responded cautiously, "I guess my father is thinking about me, I don't know."

She answered nonchalantly, "Well, it is more than a notion." This is what my mother would always say when she did not know what to say or if she refused to make a comment on a given subject.

I tried to assure my mother that I did not want to search for my father at this time. I replied, "Mom, I wanted to wait until I finished college to find my father, but it looks like I might have to do it now. Do you know where he is or where any of his family is?"

My mother's tone changed. She was very unpleasant as she stated, "Crissy, you have a father. He has raised you and he has been a good father to you."

I desperately pleaded, "Mom, I know he has been a good father, but what am I supposed to do? I am going blind. I am seeing things and I cannot take it. I do not understand what is going on with me. If my father is thinking about me this hard, then I need to do something about it so that I can concentrate on my education."

Unenthusiastically, she said, "I will think about it."

"Yes, ma'am," I said reluctantly, "I better try to get back to my school work."

I knew I had struck a nerve with her. It was time to get off the phone.

She told me unemotionally, "Ok, I will talk to you later Crissy."

Saddened, I stated, "Ok, Mom good-bye."

I could tell my mother was leery about the things I had told her. I was leery about it myself. I thought I was going crazy. I believe; if I had been in a sound Bible based church at the time, someone may have been able to help me. I was about to encounter the most difficult incident. It was one hundred times more unbelievable. I would say it was unreal, had I not lived through it myself. The following event happened a couple of weeks after I called my mother. I remember this moment as though it happened yesterday.

I started my day off as usual and went to my classes. Before the end of the first class, I developed the cramps. When I had the cramps, the pain was always unbearable, agonizing, excruciating, and intense. I did not want to eat or be around people. Because of the discomfort, I did not want to talk, walk, eat, or anything else. The pain was more than I could bear. The only thing I wanted to do was to go to bed and sleep since it allowed me to escape from my misery. I walked back to my dorm. I put my books on my desk and went to bed. I always curled myself into a ball, but today was different. I could not stay in the bed.

As soon as I reclined to relax my body, I sat up. I was not trying to get up. I wanted to rest. I strained myself with everything in my being to make myself lie down and go to bed. My body ignored me. It got up and walked to the dresser. I was puzzled, scared, and most of all, in shock. This was the first time in my life; I experienced the lack of control over my body. It resisted all of my commands.

My hand reached in my dresser drawer and pulled out a ten-dollar bill. Thinking was the only function I had. I could not speak. My conscious mind was confused. Something was controlling my body, but I did not know what. Remember, my father told God to make me come and find him. I know now that God was controlling my body. I am asking you to think outside of the box and believe in a Sovereign God. God is in control of everything that happens. The Bible says:

"But Jesus beheld them, and said unto them, With men this is impossible; but with God all things are possible."
Matthew 19:26 KJV

Here is an example of God controlling someone in His Word.

"And the Lord said unto Moses, When thou goest to return into Egypt, see that thou do all those wonders before Pharaoh, which I have put in thine hand: but I will harden his heart, and he shall not let the people go."
Exodus 14:21 KJV

From here, I will rehash the conversation I had with

my body while God controlled my every move.

I asked myself confusingly, "Why do you need ten dollars? Go back to bed please, I have the cramps."

It felt like the television show, 'Twilight Zone.' My body started walking out of my bedroom, my hand picked up my keys, and the next thing I knew, I was leaving the dorm.

Clueless, I asked, "Where are you going? I do not want to go anywhere. I am hurting too bad for this. I want to go back to bed. Why are you doing this?"

This was not making any sense to me. I was miserable. Imagine being in your body and you cannot control any of its actions. I did not understand what was happening to me.

As I was walking, I also remembered, it was a very hot day. The heat and the cramps mixed together made a bad combination. This made me extra miserable. I was still wondering where my body was taking me. What could be so important that I was not able to rest while I was feeling ill? My body walked about five blocks away and stopped at a drugstore on a corner.

Shocked at where I ended up, I inquired, "What do you want in here? I don't need anything."

My body did not go shopping. It immediately got in line.

Dumbfounded, I questioned myself, "Why are we in line? Let us go back to bed please. I am begging you to stop this. I have the cramps. Listen to me."

Of course, my body disregarded me. When it was my turn to get up to the cashier, I was astonished at what my mouth spoke.

Out of nowhere, my voice asked, "Can I have change for this ten dollar bill please?"

25

Now, I was flabbergasted and thinking, "Why do you need change? I am not going to do any laundry."

My body ignored me as the cashier gave me a roll of quarters.

Again, my voice replied politely, "Thank you."

As my body left the drugstore, it headed back towards my dormitory. I began feeling relieved that we were going back to bed; at least I thought so at the time.

I said to myself with enthusiasm, "That's it. Go back to bed. Thank you so much, let's get some rest."

My body went back to the dorm; however, it did not go back to my room. I noticed that I stopped at a pay phone. Disappointed, I said to myself, "I don't want to talk to anyone. Whom are you calling? What is wrong with you? Go back to bed please I beg you."

My hand dialed zero. I wondered, "Why do you need the operator?"

A woman pleasantly answered, "May I help you?"

With confidence, my voice asked, "Yes, can you give me the number for the Federal Penitentiary in Atlanta, Georgia please?"

For the first time, I realized what my body was doing. It was trying to find my father. I tried to correct my body. In my mind, I thought it was wrong about my father's whereabouts.

I scolded my body and countered, "My father is not in Atlanta, Georgia. He is in Iowa. What are you doing? Do you remember the 'Jet Magazine' in the fifth grade? You are calling the wrong place."

Once again, my body disregarded me and called the prison in Atlanta despite what I told it to do.

My voice explained to the guard, "Hi, my name is Crisalyn Smith. My father is in prison and his name is

James Millard Jones. I was wondering; could I have his address please? I want to write him."

A male prison guard respectfully replied, "Sure, ma'am, what did you say his name was again?"

My voice responded, "James Millard Jones."

This further confirmed, that my father was definitely the reason I was going through all of these unexplainable happenings.

The prison guard searched and answered back, "Ma'am, we don't have anyone here by that name. I am so sorry."

My voice insisted, "Are you sure?"

I thought I was clearly losing my mind. I believed I was going crazy without a doubt. Not only was my body not listening to me; it was not listening to the prison guard. None of this made any sense.

The prison guard assured me, "Yes, ma'am, I am positive."

Graciously, my voice responded, "Okay, thank you."

My hand hung up the phone. I tried to convince my body to call the Iowa Federal Penitentiary.

My body released me and I was able to call the operator to contact the prison in Iowa.

I courteously stated, "Hi, my name is Crisalyn Smith and I am looking for my father James Millard Jones. Is he there?"

A male prison guard replied, "Let me check."

Time felt like eternity as I waited for the response. All I wanted to do was to go to bed. My cramps were getting worse. The pain was all the way up my back and down to the bottom of my feet. My stomach felt like a truck ran over it. I was a hostage to my body and I knew it would retake control of me if I did not finish this phone call. Finally, the prison guard came back to the phone.

After his pursuit he explained, "Ma'am, I am so sorry, we released him years ago. I can give you his inmate number, but that is all I can do."

My heart sank. On the table by the phones, there were some pencils and paper. I wrote down my father's inmate number. Now my body took over again since it wanted to show me something else. I still found it hard to understand. What more did my body want of me? My body called back to the prison in Atlanta. I was extremely bewildered.

Baffled, I asked my body, "Why are you calling them back? They already told you that my father is not there. Why aren't you listening to anybody? What is wrong with you? Don't you see I am not feeling well?"

My body had no sympathy. It was going to do this whether I liked it or not and whether I wanted to do this or not.

The male prison guard pleasantly replied, "Atlanta Federal Penitentiary, may I help you?"

My voice nicely insisted, "Yes, could you please look for the inmate James Millard Jones one more time for me?"

The guard agreed, "Sure, hold on."

Why was my body so persistent? I did not understand. The prison guard came back to the phone.

As he searched for my father's name on the roster, I could hear him breathe. The guard told me, "Ma'am, I can't find the name you gave me anywhere."

My body's immediate response was, "Do you have the superintendent of the prison's name, phone number, and address?"

Superintendent of the prison? How did my body know to ask for someone like that? I never knew this position existed. I only knew about the warden.

The guard assertively said, "Yes, we do ma'am. Are you ready to write it?"

My hand picked up a pencil and a piece of paper while my voice responded, "Yes I am."

The guard proceeded to give me the information I needed. I was shocked with the knowledge of my body. How did it know this fact? I did not understand. I was not able to analyze the situation, as I normally could do. My body was more intelligent than I was and it ignored all of my questions. Now, my body started walking back to my room. Needless-to-say, I could not go to bed and rest. First, I had to write a letter to the superintendent. The letter went something like this:

> Dear Superintendent,
> My name is Crisalyn Smith. I am looking for my father, James Millard Jones. I called the Federal Penitentiary in Atlanta, Georgia. They told me my father was not at this facility. Could you please let me know if he is or is not in your prison system? His inmate number is what-ever-it-was. Thank you for your help in this matter.
>
> Sincerely,
> Crisalyn Smith

My hands sealed up the letter into an envelope, put a stamp on it, and then I walked to the mailbox. Once I dropped the letter into the mailbox, my body released me. I could finally go to bed; however, I could not go to sleep. I was not able to talk because I was trying to process what I had experienced for the last couple of hours. I did not know what to make of this whole ordeal.

I wished I had kept copies of the correspondences between the superintendent, my grandmother, my father, and myself to validate this story. I never thought I would find myself writing about it. The truth of the matter is; I hate to read and write. I was never going to become an author. I am an author out of obedience to God. The Word says:

"And Samuel said, Hath the Lord as great delight in burnt offerings and sacrifices, as in obeying the voice of the Lord? Behold, to obey is better than sacrifice, and to hearken than the fat of rams.
For rebellion is as the sin of witchcraft, and stubbornness is as iniquity and idolatry. Because thou hast rejected the word of the Lord, he hath also rejected thee from being king."
1 Samuel 15:22-23 KJV

I decided I had to find my father immediately. Something must be going on for me to have all of these strange unexplained episodes. My grades started to drop. I needed mental help, I thought. I went to see the psychiatrist. I explained all of these crazy events that I had experienced.

Ohio State assigned me to a female psychiatrist and she said, "What a story you have. Are you the oldest of your siblings?"

Puzzled, I answered, "Yes."

She continued to ask, "How many siblings do you have?"

I replied, "Six."

She intellectually explained, "Well, I think you are worried about your siblings; so subconsciously this is your way of dealing with the fact you are not there to care for them."

Frustrated, I said, "Ma'am, this doesn't have anything to do with my siblings. This has to do with my biological father. I am here to figure out how to deal with this stuff and keep up my grades. I do not have time to worry about my siblings. That is what my parents are for, that is their job. My job is to pass school. I am asking you; how do I handle what is going on with me at the same time I try to keep my grades from failing?"

The psychiatrist calmly expounded, "I am telling you, you still feel responsible for your siblings. You may not think that you are, but you are."

With frustration I stated, "Okay, I am leaving."

The psychiatrist asked, "Do you want another appointment? You need one you know."

I rebelled her opinion and insisted, "No, you are not listening. This has nothing to do with my siblings. I am glad I do not have to take care of my siblings or be responsible for them at this time in my life. I will find a way to deal with this on my own."

I left her office. As I looked back now, I did the right thing. One thing did not have anything to do with the other. I believe Satan was trying to make me believe something that was not happening. I did not realize it at that moment; however, I realize it today. I was not in tune with God spiritually; nevertheless, I had an analytical mind. My thoughts did not except anything the psychiatrist told me.

I called my mother once again because I was hoping that maybe she would believe me this time.

My spirit was broken and I told her, "Something else happened Mom. I am troubled and I do not know what to do."

I proceeded to tell her the story about my inner body experience. She could hardly believe her ears.

My mother was stunned and could not comfort me. She unbelievingly stated, "Well, Crissy, I don't know what to tell you. Are you sure, you were not dreaming? Some dreams seem real, you know."

With my back against the wall, and out of hopelessness, I answered, "Mom, if you don't believe me, no one will. I am calling because it is time to find my father now because I want everything to stop. Do you know where his mother or anyone in his family is?"

My mother finally felt my pain and realized she could not help me. I could tell she wanted to help but she did not know how to help her child. Not to mention, she was still dealing with her pain and anger from her past concerning my father. My mother said the only things she knew to say, "No, and I don't want to know where they are. You are on your own. You don't have to let this control you."

I downheartedly responded, "I have tried to let it go. My grades are failing. I have done all that I can do. Mom, I could not make my body do anything. What am I supposed to do?"

My mother had now changed her tone. I was hurting her unintentionally. I needed her, but I knew the time was coming for me to leave the bird's nest. I was going to have to accomplish this task on my own even though I did not want to depart from my mother's security. I realized that I did not have her blessing anymore and I did not want to keep hurting her emotionally.

My mother unsympathetically replied, "I don't know what to tell you. You are hurting us. I don't understand why you want to find someone who has not taken care of you."

With stress, I answered, "Mom, and I don't understand why I could not control my body. I don't know why I became blind and saw those crazy things. I just want all of this to go away."

She asked me once again, "Are you sure your imagination isn't playing tricks on you?"

I insisted, "If it is, it sure is doing a great job. Well, I got to go Mom, thanks a lot."

As I look back at this conversation, my mother did not recognize the spirit of the Lord. A few years later, my mother could distinguish the voice of God. Unfortunately, at this time, she was not able to help me differentiate that I was dealing with my heavenly Father. The Bible says:

"Hereby know ye the Spirit of God: Every spirit that confesseth that Jesus Christ is come in the flesh is of God."
1 John 4:2 KJV

In addition, it states:

"My sheep hear my voice, and I know them, and they follow me:"
John 10:27 KJV

I had no idea that God was communicating with me. I

did not recognize His Spirit moving me towards this path. I was lost in sin, even though I had a good and kind heart. I was not serving the Lord with my life. I was partying because of my newfound freedom from a strict home. I was not going to church and I hardly ever prayed. God evidently did not care about my lifestyle. He was trying to reach me and I did not connect the dots.

I began searching for James Millard Jones on my own. I contacted some people who I knew in Xenia, Ohio. They referred me to some of my father's old time friends. During my search for my father, some people told me he was dead. I knew that a dead person could not send me through all of these extraordinary changes. I did not accept their answer even though they were apologetic while they were trying to comfort me at the same time. I especially knew a dead person could not control a body like what I had experienced. I remembered a pastor preaching this:

"For the living know that they shall die: but the dead know not any thing, neither have they any more a reward; for the memory of them is forgotten."
Ecclesiastes 9:5 KJV

Surprisingly, my mother called me back a few days later. She was in a very good disposition. She replied, "Hey Crissy. How are you?"

I answered, "I am fine Mom. What about you?"

She gleefully said, "I am fine. I got some information for you. I have your paternal-grandmother's address and phone number."

Shocked, I inquired, "What? I thought you were not

going to help me find my father."

She sternly answered, "I wasn't, but I ran into someone who had her information and they gave it to me."

I appreciatively told her, "Thanks Mom."

Again, God orchestrated this divine meeting to help me find my father. Everything was lining up perfectly; however, I did not get this revelation until I wrote this book. When I hung up the phone with my mother, I contacted my father's mother. It would be the first time I was in contact with her since I was in the second grade. I was nervous and excited at the same time.

My grandmother answered the phone.

I fretfully explained, "My name is Crisalyn Smith. My name used to be Jones but through adoption, my name changed. James Millard Jones is my father. Do you know where I can find him?"

As she became irate, she complained, "Yes, I do, but did you say you are not a Jones anymore? Why would you change your name?"

Frantically, I tried to explain, "I was just a kid and I had no choice. I was in the third grade. Nothing can change blood, no matter what your name is."

She was not happy at all with this information. "I do not know if I should give you your father's address or not. I will have to talk this over with my daughter."

"Wow, I have an aunt," I thought. I needed to contact her too, and then I will know who I am. I respectfully asked, "Can I have my aunt's number too?"

She countered, "Sure."

My grandmother proceeded to give me the number. We said our goodbyes and I called my aunt. The number was busy for fifteen minutes. When I finally got through, I was uneasy talking to my aunt for the first time in my life.

My aunt picked up the telephone.

I was just as tense as I could be, but I respectfully replied, "Auntie, my name is Crisalyn…"

She cut me short and acknowledged, "I know who you are. Mom called me."

I reluctantly requested, "Well, I was wondering if I could get my father's address. I want to write him."

Sternly my aunt responded, "No, we decided that we are not going to give you his information. But give me your address and phone number in case we change our minds."

Wounded, I questioned, "Why? That is my father. I don't understand."

Since she was the oldest sibling, she wanted to protect her brother. She firmly stated, "This may be too much for him. It is best to leave it like it is."

I gave my information to my aunt. I was hurt. I was so close to getting my father's address, but yet so far away from knowing his whereabouts. Why was everyone blocking me from my father? I did not comprehend. I got off the phone, went to my room, and cried.

Two weeks later, I received some special mail. I could not believe my eyes. The superintendent of the prisons in the state of Georgia wrote me. I also had a letter surprisingly from my grandmother. I decided to open the superintendent's letter first.

Dear Crisalyn Smith,
    Thank you for your correspondence concerning James Millard Jones. I was able to

locate him at the Federal Penitentiary here in Atlanta, Georgia. His inmate number is whatever-it-was and his address is whatever-it-was. If you need me for any other assistance or any questions, please feel free to contact me. Good luck with your father.

Best regards,
Superintendent

My mouth dropped. I could hardly believe it. My body was right. My father was where my body called in the first place. How did my body know this? This was unbelievable and incredible. This reminds me of this Bible verse:

"For there is nothing covered, that shall not be revealed; neither hid, that shall not be known."
Luke 12:2 KJV

God is omniscience and He knows everything. No one can hide or keep anything from the Lord. Many years later, I discovered He revealed my father's whereabouts through controlling my body. However, I did not know this at the time. I stood in my room with tears of joy in my eyes. I was overwhelmed that I had my father's address. It was astonishing to see that my body was right. I wondered why the prison guards could not find any record of my father. Yet, my body disclosed the information by allowing me to contact the superintendent. Next, I proceeded to open my grandmother's letter. She wrote:

Dear Crisalyn,
We were deeply hurt about your adoption and last name change. We decided to go ahead and give you your father's address. Maybe we can see each other one day. Here is your father's address.

Take care,
My paternal grandmother

In my mind, I thought, "I already have it now, it is too late."

The fact is, it wasn't too late. God confirmed my father's whereabouts on the same day that He gave me this revelation. I did not think of it as a confirmation; however, that is exactly what it was. I have to give God every bit of the credit that He deserves. He was in control of this whole ordeal. God is so awesome and perfect. I praise His holy name for He is worthy.

It was time to write my father. I could not contact the rest of the family until I had reached out to my father. I immediately wrote him and my letter read something like this:

Dear Mr. James Millard Jones,
You do not know who I am but I know who you are. My mother's name is whatever-it-was. My name is Crisalyn Smith but I was born a Jones. I am writing because I wanted to find you. I hope to hear back from you. Take care.

Love your daughter,
Crisalyn Smith

I did not know what to say really, so I wrote enough to break the ice. I instantly walked to the mailbox to mail this letter. I was so anxious to see if he would write me back and I hoped that he would not reject me. Waiting for his letter was like waiting for eternity.

When my father received my letter, he was very curious. He wondered, "Who is this and why is she writing me?" Even though he knew my name was Crisalyn, because of the fact the last name was not Jones, he did not realize I was his daughter. Once he read the letter, he knew whom I was. He was in total shock. He forgot about the letter he wrote God. Because of this, he did not connect the dots that the Lord had answered his prayer. He immediately wrote me. In one week, I received a letter from my father. His response went something like this:

> Dear Crisalyn,
>   I do know who you are. You are my daughter. I do not like your name change. It is too late to do anything about it. Nevertheless, I will say, I am so happy that you decided to contact me and I hope to see you one day. Please keep in touch because I would love to hear from you.
>
> Love your father,
> James Millard Jones

I was in shock. I was stunned. I finally had some communication with my biological father. I did not know what to do with myself. By this time, I was coming into my finals at Ohio State. With all of this commotion going on, I found it difficult to stay focused on my studies. My grade point average for that quarter dropped down to one point seven. After all, so much had happened. However, I finally found my father.

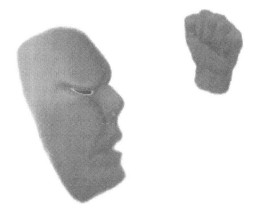

MEETING MY FATHER

It was now fall quarter. The leaves were turning to the beautiful fall colors of red, orange, yellow, and brown. It was great to be in Buckeye country. The football spirit was in the atmosphere. This school is where I learned how to be a Buckeye Fan. When I first arrived at Ohio State, I did not realize the magnitude of being an enthusiast. I was too busy being overwhelmed about finally leaving my parents and being on my own. After settling down, I began to become a real Buckeye. I am still a fan today. I am writing this book the year the Buckeyes won the National Championship in the first playoffs. Go Buckeyes! Now, I need to get back to the story.

Two weeks before God gave me this book, 'I Hate God,' He revealed a powerful word to me. The Lord gave me this in the Bible:

I Hate God

"And it shall come to pass, if thou shalt hearken diligently unto the voice of the Lord thy God, to observe and to do all his commandments which I command thee this day, that the Lord thy God will set thee on high above all nations of the earth;

And all these blessings shall come on thee, and overtake thee, if thou shalt hearken unto the voice of the Lord thy God.

Blessed shalt thou be in the city, and blessed shalt thou be in the field.

Blessed shall be the fruit of thy body, and the fruit of thy ground, and the fruit of thy cattle, the increase thy kine, and the flocks of thy sheep.

Blessed shall be thy basket and thy store.

Blessed shalt thou be when thou comest in, and blessed shalt thou be when thou goest out.

The Lord shall cause thine enemies that rise up against thee to be smitten before thy face: they shalt come out against thee one way, and flee before thee seven ways.

The Lord shall command the blessing upon thee in thy storehouses, and in all that thou settest thine hand unto; and he shall bless thee in the land which the Lord thy God giveth thee.

The Lord shall establish thee a holy people unto himself, as he hath sworn unto thee, if thou shalt keep the commandments of the Lord thy God, and walk in his ways.

And all the people of the earth shall see that thou art called by the name of the Lord; and they shall be afraid of thee.

And the Lord shall make thee plenteous in goods, in the fruit of thy body, and in the fruit of thy cattle, and in the fruit of thy ground, in the land which the Lord sware

unto thy fathers to give thee.
The Lord shall open unto thee his good treasure, the
heaven to give the rain unto thy land in his season, and
to bless all the word of thine hand: and thou shalt lend
unto many nations, and thou shalt not borrow.
And the Lord shall make thee the head, and not the tail:
and thou shalt be above only, and thou shalt not be
beneath; if that thou hearken unto the commandments of
the Lord thy God, which I command thee this day, to
observe and to do them:
And thou shalt not go aside from any of the words which
I command thee this day, to the right hand, or to the left,
to go after other gods to serve them."
Deuteronomy 28:1-14 KJV

God had given this to the Israelites after spending
forty years in the wilderness for their disobedience. I did
not take this message lightly after hearing two ministers
preach about it in two different cities and four days apart
of each other. These preachers had never met and their
sermons were practically identical. I had confirmation
and I began to wait on the Lord. I knew I was going to
have to obey God and do something. Soon after these
messages, I knew just what He wanted me to do. I had to
write this book. I did not want to author a book with a
controversial title; however, I still had to obey the will
of the Lord.

Forty years is significant in my life and this
testimony. Forty years ago from, March 2015, my father
put a letter in a tree to God. July of 2015, forty years
ago, I had those crazy visions and inner body
experiences. January of 2016 marks forty years for
meeting my father for the first time. Funny how this

timing is so perfect in correlation to the writing of this book. God's timing is always perfect.

My Timeline of Forty Years

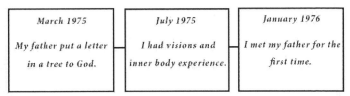

March 1975	July 1975	January 1976
My father put a letter in a tree to God.	I had visions and inner body experience.	I met my father for the first time.

My father and I kept in contact while I was still in school. My concentration improved as I focused on my studies. Being in touch with my father was still a distraction in my schooling. If this had been just a couple of years later, the timing would have been more convenient for me. Life is not always about convenience. I moved into an apartment right off of campus. This made it easier for my father to contact me. He could call me collect from prison. Our conversations were short but we were slowly getting to know each other.

Around December of 1975, he began to want me to come and visit him. The phone rang and it was my father.

He asked eagerly, "How are you Daughter?"

This is the nickname that my father calls me to this day. He very rarely calls me Crisalyn or Crissy.

I was happy to hear from him. I replied, "I am fine Dad. How are you?"

He said jokingly, "I would be better if I were not in here."

He chuckled with a flamboyant voice. When my father laughed, it was as though I heard my own voice in a deeper tone. The way we laugh is very similar. Therefore, whenever he laughed, I laughed and visa-

44

versa. He still tells jokes all of the time as we constantly laugh at each other.

He became composed and said, "I was wondering if you would like to come here to Atlanta to visit me?"

Wow, my father wanted me to visit him. I waited all of my life for this. I enthusiastically responded, "Sure Dad, but I don't have any money while I am in school right now. It will have to wait until I finish college."

My father assured me, "I will get you the money. I do not want to wait that long. So if I get you the money, will you come?"

I could not argue this valid point. I did not want to dispute it because I really wanted to go see him. I inquired, "When did you want me to come there Dad?"

He probed, "How about next month?"

I concurred quickly and stated, "Okay, if you get me the money Dad, I will come."

Breathlessly my father replied, "I will get on it right away. My wife will be contacting you. She will pay for your trip."

I eagerly agreed, "Okay Dad, I will come if someone pays for my trip."

A few days later, my father called and he was upset. He sounded like he had lost his best friend. I knew something was wrong.

He was in a state of hopelessness and said, "Hey Daughter, I have bad news."

I was apprehensive and asked, "What's wrong Dad?"

Sounding depressed, he replied, "The people here at the prison said you can't come see me unless you have a birth certificate proving that I am your father."

I was not going to let him stay down in the dumps. The information I had would cheer him up and I assured him saying, "Dad, I can get my original birth certificate from my mother. I will call her. She said I could have it when I grew up, so that won't be a problem."

Feeling like there was hope, he said, "I sure hope so because if you don't, you won't be able to come."

I hastily added, "I will call Mom right now."

My father responded, "Okay, I will call you back if they let me. Otherwise, I will call you back as soon as I can."

I immediately called my mother.

I instantly asked her, "Mom, I was wondering if I could have my birth certificate that you told me I could have when I grew up. I need it to go see my father in prison."

My mother abruptly countered, "No."

Puzzled and shocked at my mother's response, I questioned, "But why Mom? I won't be able to see my father without it."

She was very blunt, "I burnt it. No."

Wounded, I answered, "Man, I don't know what I am going to do. I really need my birth certificate."

She straightforwardly responded, "Well, I don't have it."

Sadden, I replied, "Okay, thanks Mom. I will figure out something."

I cried when I hung up the phone. I began to try to think about and analyze the situation. I thought, "Now what can I do?"

As I was going back and forward in my mind, suddenly, a light bulb lit up in my head. I needed to write the superintendent another letter. He had told me if I had any more problems to contact him. Therefore, I immediately wrote him and the letter sounded something like this:

> Dear Mr. Superintendent,
>   My name is Crisalyn Smith. I was trying to see my father, James Millard Jones whatever-his-inmate-number-was. The guards at the prison told my father that he could not see me without my birth certificate with his name on it. In the third grade, I went through the adoption process. I had no choice. For seventy-five years, those records are sealed. My mother told me she burnt up my original birth certificate so I do not have any way of proving I am who I say I am. Could you please make an exception so that I can see my father? I have waited all my life to meet him. I would appreciate any help in this matter. Thank you again for helping me to meet my father.
>
> Sincerely,
> Crisalyn Smith

I mailed the letter and waited. My father called me back and I told him the situation. He was angry because my mother destroyed my birth certificate. I told him that I wrote a letter to the superintendent. I assured him that everything would be okay. We would have to wait until I heard back from the superintendent.

About a week and a half later, I received a letter from the superintendent.

> Dear Crisalyn Smith,
>   I can understand your position. I am going to grant you permission to see your father, James

Millard Jones. I will put your name on his list.
Bring this letter with you and show it to the
guard. If you have any problems, my number is
xxx-xx-xxxx. I hope your visit with your father
goes well.

Sincerely,
Mr. Superintendent

I was so happy and relieved. I could not wait for my
father to call me. He called me a few days later after I
received the letter.

Dad was feeling down in the dumps. He said, "Hey
Daughter."

I knew his spirit would change. I responded, "Hey
Dad. I got great news."

Sounding hopeful he asked, "Did the superintendent
write you?"

Excitedly, I replied, "Yes and he said he is giving his
permission for me to see you. He also said to call him if
I have any problems when I come. He told me to enjoy
my visit with you."

My father was thrilled and responded, "I will call my
wife and tell her to send you the money. I cannot wait to
see you. Can you try to come January the twenty-forth?"

Happy to know we had some enjoyment for a few
minutes, I countered, "Yes I can. I will try."

No one could stop me from seeing my father
anymore and I was glad the many years of pain were
ending. The agony of not being able to know my full
identity was excruciating. I needed to know; who is
Crisalyn?

Wow, now that I knew I was going to see my father

soon, I was just as scared as I was excited. His wife did contact me and sent me the money to go to Atlanta in January. I made the reservations. Nothing was as easy as I thought it would be. My parents were not happy that I was going to see my father. They also were not happy that I was going to Georgia alone. My mother called me and she did not have anything good to say.

My mother asked me with a disturbed voice, "Hey Crissy, are you busy?"

I replied, "No, ma'am."

She continued firmly, "I have been thinking about this excursion of yours. You do not need to go to Atlanta. I want you to cancel the trip."

I did not have a choice in my mind or heart. I had to go. I countered, "Mom, I need to go. I want to go. They have already paid for my trip."

She became angry and told me, "It is too dangerous. I am telling you, you don't need to go."

I did not want to talk about this with my mother because I knew how she felt about my father. I calmly replied, "Mom, I have to go."

She was not going to settle with my answer, she sternly insisted, "No you don't. If something happens to you, we will not be able to afford to help you. If you die, we won't be able to send for your body."

Feeling defeated at the same time liberated, I replied, "Mom, if I die, I will not care where my body is."

I could not believe the resistance I was getting from my mother. Since I was paying my own way through college, paying for my rent, and paying for my food, I figured it was time for me to grow up and stick to my decision. I did not want to hurt my parents, but I did. My father and I had been hurt all of these years. They had

I Hate God

blocked us from seeing each other. To my father, it was as though they buried me alive and hid me from his reach.

I remembered when I was in the third grade, my father tried to visit me in Springfield, Ohio. He came all the way from Cedar Rapids, Iowa to see me. He went to see my maternal grandmother and grandfather in Xenia, Ohio. He asked them where Mom and I were. They told him that they did not know when in fact they were acquainted with our whereabouts. My father went to visit more of my relatives and received the same answer. He drove to Dayton, where his mother lived and went back to Xenia to see if he could find any of my mother's friends. He finally found a friend who knew that my mother moved to Springfield. This became his next destination.

Once my father arrived to Springfield, he began to ask people questions concerning my mother's whereabouts. In conclusion, he ran into someone who knew my mother. They did not know her address, but they knew the street she lived on at the time. My father and his wife started knocking at every door on the street. By now, it is nine o'clock at night. He had spent the whole day looking for me. When he arrived at our door, things got nasty.

My mother was pregnant. She was not in the mood to let my father come visit me. She did not care what he had gone through that day. She did not care how far away he traveled. Most of all, she did not want to get me out of the bed to see him. He was angry and one of the neighbors called the police. I was awake through all of this, but I did not know it was my father at the door. They arrested my father and he spent the night in jail.

The next morning, my mother reluctantly said, "Crissy, I need to tell you something."

I did not know what to expect and asked, "What is it Mama?"

She questioned me, "Do you know who was at the door last night?"

I replied, "No, ma'am, who?"

She said with a sigh, "Your father."

Shocked, I asked, "My father?"

I did not understand why I did not get to see him. What happened? I was puzzled.

My mother assured me, "Yes, your father."

Not knowing the situation, I asked, "Why didn't he see me then?"

She seemed to be slightly irritated and responded, "Because he came too late and I didn't feel like getting you up."

Crushed by this whole thing, I countered, "But I wasn't asleep Mama. Why don't you want me to see my father? My stepsiblings were able to see their mother real late at night. Why couldn't I see my father?"

I had tears swelling in my eyes until they began to roll down my face. My mother could see the hurt she had caused me as she continued her conversation.

Abruptly she said, "Well, I didn't let him and that is that. I told him he had to come back today. He caused such a ruckus last night that the police came and arrested him. He spent the night in jail."

It traumatized me to know my father spent the night in jail. Without knowing the rest of the story, I knew this was wrong. As a child, I could not do anything. I inquired, "My father went to jail last night?"

Reluctantly my mother told me, "Yes, they are letting

him out today (Saturday) so he might come back to see you."

With a spark of hope, I asked, "He might come back?"

She halfheartedly said, "Yes, so don't be surprised if he does."

To this day, I do not understand why my mother did not let me see my father. I needed to see him. Even in the third grade, I knew my father was a victim of wrong doings. I waited all day to see him. My heart was aching because my father never came. It was not until I was older that I would understand why he did not return.

Now, I had to make a decision. I had to make a fair decision to my father and to myself. After having all of those blind and inner body experiences, I was not willing to repeat these occurrences. After my father stressed how he wanted to see me, I was not willing to make him wait any longer. Eighteen years had passed since he had last seen me. It was time, so I took the trip. I was uncertain either way it went but I had to go. It was my destiny. The Bible says:

"For I know the thoughts that I think toward you, saith the Lord, thoughts of peace, and not of evil, to give you an expected end."
Jeremiah 29:11 KJV

This was my first airplane flight. I was scared to death; however, I still had to do it. I had to be brave and be adventurous. I let the fact that I wanted to fix my eyes on my father's face be my dominant factor. I boarded the plane. The takeoff was not comfortable. As we ascended into the sky, my ears were popping. It was somewhat painful. After getting into the air, I began to settle down a little when they offered me something to eat and drink. When we began to descend, I was glad to see the ground. I finally traveled to a state other than Ohio, Kentucky, Illinois, and Indiana. I arrived in Atlanta, Georgia.

I picked up my bags and I saw the signs pointing to where the cabs were. I got in the first one. I told the cab driver to take me to the hotel closest to the Federal Penitentiary and he did. I checked into the hotel. I dropped my bags in the room. I settled myself down for a few minutes. When I was ready, I called another taxi to come and take me to the prison. It was not long before my transportation was in front of the hotel. I was moments away from seeing my father for the very first time.

When I arrived at the prison, I remember feeling out of place. This part did not matter; I had to do what I came to accomplish. I went through too much and traveled too far to turn back now; it was too late. I was into this thing all the way. I walked through the door straight to the guard's desk. I stared at the bars in disbelief. They were tan square bars just as I saw in the visions. The guard signed me in and opened the first section of the prison corridor.

As I walked down the hallway, the bars behind me closed with a loud boom. The prisoners were saying nasty and vulgar things to me. It was more than I could handle. I just focused on the fact that I had to see my father. I went through the second set of bars and again the cell doors made a loud boom behind me. There was my father outside of the family room waiting to see me. He introduced himself.

With a half-smile on his face, my father said, "Hi Daughter, it's me, your father."

I nervously replied, "Hi Dad."

He nodded his head towards the room, directed me to go in, and said, "Let's go in here and get a table."

I agreed, "Okay."

Before we sat down at the table, my father hugged and kissed me. He had something to ask me.

He wanted me to know whom I was dealing with and probed, "I painted one of these pictures around here on the wall. Do you know which one Daughter?"

The four walls around the room were loaded with pictures. I saw the picture that was in my vision. I did not want my vision to be right about the painting because I did not want to believe my father had that much hatred in his heart. I pointed to a beautiful scenery picture first.

He replied bluntly, "No."

I pointed to another picture of some beautiful flowers.

He was firm with his answer, "No, but you know which one I painted, don't you?"

Unfortunately, I did in fact know. I unwillingly knew I had to point to the correct picture in my vision and replied, "Yes, sir."

How did he know I knew which image he painted? It was time to point to the portrait in my vision. It was right behind me. I turned around and pointed to it reluctantly.

Inquisitively he probed, "Now why didn't you point to that picture in the first place?"

Looking down at the floor with shyness, I responded, "Because I did not want to accept that you painted the most hateful painting in here."

My father boldly justified, "Well, I did. Now, have a seat. I need to tell you something."

We sat down and what came out of my father's mouth was quite painful.

His mannerism transformed right before my eyes. His hateful raging spirit surfaced and he told me, "First of all, I hate God. I hate my mother. I hate my father. I hate my sister. I hate your mother and her husband. I hate your grandfather. I hate your grandmother. I hate your great grandmother," (then putting more emphasis on the rest of his statement he said), "and I hate you."

I was a very sensitive person. If my father had not said he hated God first, his mother second, and the rest of the lineup on down to me, I probably would have cried. However, seeing that I am not God or his mother, I thought, "Who am I?"

He continued to ask, "Why did you come here? Why did you contact me? You are your mother's spy, aren't you?"

Shocked I replied, "You asked me to come. No, I am not Mom's spy. She did not want me to see you. I am here against her wishes."

Looking doubtful my father responded, "I don't believe you. I think she sent you here to spy on me to rub it in my face that I am serving time."

I was not expecting our visit to be on such a negative note. I was hurt and insisted, "Dad, my parents at home are angry with me. I am struggling at school to keep up my grades. You paid for my trip and you think I am a spy? Why would you pay for a spy to come and see you?"

He maintained his position and responded, "I just

wanted to meet you, but I know that you are spying on me for your mother."

I could not convince my father that I was not a spy for my mother. I was uncomfortable, but I knew I had to stay. After all, where could I go? I decided to stay and use the allotted time granted to see my father. It did not matter if the time was good or bad. It was hours I never had with my father. When visiting hours were over, I went back to the hotel.

That night, I heard one of the most powerful sermons in my life on the radio. I was trying to find a station with soul music.

I could not continue to turn the station because once I heard the preacher say, "What in Hell do you want?" I was stuck and had to finish hearing the rest of the sermon.

I was like, "Wow, what is he preaching?" I had to listen to this.

The preacher continued to say, "You are not going to want a chair to sit down. Why? You will be too hot to sit down. You are not going to want to party. Why? You will be too hot to party."

I was not a type of person to shout at any sermons, but I found myself shouting at this message on the radio.

Not realizing the Holy Spirit was present, I shouted, "Amen. Preach."

This was not my normal character. The sermon was on fire. I was getting motivated after the painful day at the penitentiary.

The minister preached, "You are not going to want to eat. Why? You will be too hot to eat. You are not going to want to laugh and talk. Why? You will be too hot to laugh and talk. Get yourself right before it is too late.

What in Hell do you want? I am telling you, you don't want anything in the pits of Hell."

I continued to shout, "Yeah, amen."

After the sermon was over, I was able to turn on some soul music. I was uncomfortable at the hotel because I felt lonely. This was my first trip where no one was with me. I went to bed and I soon drifted off to sleep with that powerful sermon on my mind.

The next day, I went back to see my father before I departed Atlanta. He had special permission for me to see him one more time. This get-together went a little better than our first visit. We had a much better conversation.

My father greeted me with humiliation, "Hi Daughter, I want you to know how you are embarrassing me."

I was very puzzled. How in the world did I shame my father?

With a questioning frown, I asked, "How did I do that Dad?"

Firmly he asked, "Do you feel the temperature that it is outside?"

Not knowing what he was getting at, I said, "Yes, it is about seventy degrees."

He countered, as he was blushing, "Look at what you are wearing. Everyone is making fun of me because of how you are dressed. Why do you have on all of those heavy outrageous hot clothes?"

I had on a long wool skirt, a turtleneck sweater, and some fashionable boots. I started laughing as I was sweating. I was embarrassed and countered, "Well, Dad, it was snowing and freezing cold in Ohio when I left. This is January. I thought it was winter everywhere. I have never gone anywhere outside of the northern states. This is my first time that I traveled to the south. I did not know. Trust me; I am burning up with these clothes. Don't you see me sweating?"

My father laughed when he saw I was laughing at myself. It was nice to see this side of him. He started cracking jokes about me. "Well, I want you to know, when they make fun of you to me, I don't know you and I am going to make fun of you too. I am going to tell them that you are a mad woman."

My father found it easier to communicate with me by cracking jokes. Little did he know, I was ready and willing to accept his challenge. I was used to making jokes about my own self. Therefore, I decided to crack some jokes about me too, and retaliated as I said, "Well, I wore my coat down here Dad. I could have worn that in here too, then what?"

My father laughed even harder and replied, "I would have told the guards, she isn't my daughter, that's an imposter. Don't ever come here dressed like that again Daughter. I promise you; you will not get inside of the gate. You look ridiculous."

We joked about my clothes until I had to leave. I laughed so hard until my stomach hurt and I was crying with laughter. The more he talked, the more I laughed at myself. I realized from this moment, my father was, and still is a comedian. At least we were laughing even though I was the center of his humiliating topic. I could handle this much better than the hate conversations. Over the years, I would always reflect back to the very first time I met my father.

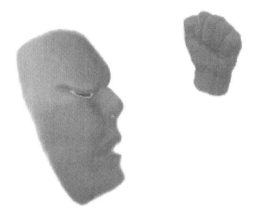

ANGRY WITH GOD

Many years had passed and I was now married with two children. The marriage was very miserable because of physical and mental abuse. One day I sat in my living room while I was angry with my husband, the world, and God. I took my anger out on my children who were two and three years old. My son was the oldest. Their names were Bob J and Thiess. My children were in my son's room, minding their own business, and playing together. They were quiet and their behavior was extremely good. I, on the other hand, was in the living room watching television. I had my head in my hand with my arm on the armrest of the couch. You could see the steam coming out my ears if you looked hard enough at me.

I noticed the children were too quiet. I went back to Bob J's bedroom and saw them playing. My son was helping Thiess. They were building something. This did not stop what I did next. I yelled at the top of my lungs. "What are you doing?"

I startled them. Bob J had this gift of analyzing people. If my son was not scared, my daughter was not alarmed. My son, without fear in a deep monotone voice, calmly said, "We are just playing Mama. We're being good."

I furiously growled, "Oh."

I walked away as I was still fuming. I went to the living room and continued thinking about all of the events from the previous night. As I thought about these things, I became angrier and angrier. About fifteen minutes later, I decided to go back and yell at the kids.

I angrily roared, "What are you doing now?"

My son courageously replied peacefully, "We are still being good Mama. See, we are still playing."

I evilly snarled, "Oh."

Bob J was smiling even though he saw I had an ugly irritated face. He was able to look beyond my outer appearance. My children continued playing and I went back to my spot in the living room. Nothing was calming me down. I did not know what to do, but I was going to do something. In the meantime, I kept on being irate. After about fifteen more minutes, I went back to my son's room.

I continued to torment my children and screamed, "What are you doing now?"

Bob J and Thiess looked up at me again with strange faces. They remained calm and my son assured me serenely, "Mama, we are still being good. See?"

I grouchily puffed, "Oh."

This time I stormed away with more rage. I was not going to cool down any time soon. I went back to my spot on the couch. I did not even try to control this anger. God only knows where this rage was going to lead if I did not get a grip. This time was different. My children came to me a few minutes later. Bob J led the way. He was Thiess' protector. The truth is; he was my protector. Whenever my daughter spoke, she had a soft Mickey Mouse voice. My son was practically in my face on the same side of the couch I was sitting.

Bob J boldly began to say, "Mama."

As anger was raging in my heart, I did not give my child a motherly response. I immediately screeched, "What?"

He curiously asked, "Mama, can me and Thiess ask you an important question?"

I remember thinking, "What kind of question would be important from a three year old?"

My response still was not kind. It was full of fury; however, it was a reaction and the only one I could give.

I roared even louder, "What?"

This had no effect on Bob J or Thiess as I grumbled at them. Thiess was a sensitive child except for when her brother assured her everything was all right no matter how things appeared.

Bob J continued, "Well, me and Thiess want to know, do you have a problem or something?"

At this time, I felt crunchy. I felt like I was one inch tall. I was guilty as charged and I was so ashamed. My anger was smaller than my sins against my children. I began to falter.

Embarrassed and humiliated about my behavior I stuttered, "Ah… ah… ah… Yes, I got a problem."

My child looked pleased that he had just figured out what was wrong. He assured himself, his sister, and me, everything was okay.

He calmly replied, "I thought so, because you keep on yelling at us for no reason. You should yell at us if you got a problem. So Mama, keep on yelling at us because we know you got a problem."

Then he turned to his sister and said, "Mama got a problem."

Thiess repeated her brother the best she could and replied, "Mama problem?"

He confirmed, "Yes, Mama got a problem. So we are going to go back and play, but Mama is going to come back there and yell at us some more. Okay?"

She reiterated, "Okay."

My son turned back to me and stated, "Mama, well, we know you got a problem. You just keep on yelling at us and we will keep on playing and being good. You come back and yell at us all you want because you got a problem."

Then he turned to his sister and said, "Come on Thiess, let's go back and play because we are going to keep on being good and Mama is going to keep yelling at us because she has a problem."

As my children went back to my son's room, I felt so bad and I began to ask myself, "What are you doing Crisalyn? Why are you yelling at good children?"

After about a half hour, I mustered up the strength and courage to apologize to my children. My son did not make this process easy; however, I deserved every word he told me.

As Bob J prepared Thiess, he whispered, "Here comes Mama, she is going to yell at us. Okay?"

Thiess whispered, "Okay."

Little did they know; I was coming to do the

complete opposite. I was going to make the wrong that I had done right.

I spoke to them with tenderness in my voice. I softly said, "Hey you guys, I am so sorry for yelling at you. I won't yell at you anymore; you have been good all day."

Assuring me once again, Bob J replied, "Mama, we know you got a problem so you just keep on yelling at us. We know we are being good. You should yell at us if you got a problem. So it's okay, yell at us all you want because you got a problem."

What can I say? They were stuck in one mind-set. They were giving me permission to yell at them. My children were okay with it. Since this made me feel worse and my apology was difficult to do, I left and never went back to my son's room. Most of all, I became angry with myself for my behavior to innocent little children. As for God, I was still angry with Him for a few more years.

As I look back at this story, I treated my children in the same way I did God. I was angry with all of them and none of them did anything to me. The Word says:

"Let all bitterness, and wrath, and anger, and clamor, and evil speaking, be put away from you, with all malice:"
Ephesians 4:31 KJV

Why was I angry? My husband had beaten me. The more I prayed, the more my husband beat and mistreated me. I figured God did not love me because He was not answering my prayers. This was my biggest error. The mistake was blaming my situation on God. I did not know about spiritual warfare. I did not know how to fight it. I hated to read so I barely read the Bible. I might have picked up the Bible two or three times a year. This was not enough of God's Word in my life. I did not know it, but my soul was hungry and it needed spiritual nutrition. I starved my existence of spiritual food. I neglected to take care of my salvation. At this time in my life, I was truly lost in the wilderness. This was the beginning of my adulterous life. I was searching for love. It was the wrong kind of love.

In the past, I backslid and turned away from God after my first three marriages. I became angry with God and I asked Him, "God don't I deserve love and a husband? What did I do that You are not giving me a good husband even after I prayed to You? Why did I get a sign from You to get married when it turned out to be painful? I do not understand Lord. Please help me." After the forth marriage, I did not backslide and I remain faithful to God even though my prayers were unanswered.

I cried many nights and throughout the day. The fourth and last time I lost a husband, it practically killed me. I became extremely depressed; however, I kept praying. I did not get angry with God. I went into the deepest depression someone could feel. I felt like a boulder rock was on me. This time, I kept holding on to God, no matter what was happening. I praised the Lord. I fasted. I prayed harder than I have ever prayed in my life. I read the Word and gained spiritual growth. I joined a spirit-filled church, which gave me strength to endure through my tribulations.

My son saved my life by coming to get me. Even though I was still depressed, I began to heal with the new surroundings in a new state. God began to teach me how to get out of depression. He began to elevate my spiritual life. I became a minister and He put different people in my path who helped me to grow.

I went to a church where I joined an organized group of people who tried to help others to get out of their depression. The sermons at the church were strong and God was teaching me something. He taught me, "My saints are depressed. Why? Where is the joy of the Lord?"

I was one of the depressed saints. The Word says:

"Then he said unto them, Go your way, eat the fat, and drink the sweet, and send portions unto them for whom nothing is prepared: for this day is holy unto our Lord: neither be ye sorry; for the joy of the Lord is your strength."
Nehemiah 8:10 KJV

I did not want to join the group, but God put it on my heart to do this. I asked God, "How can I help the depressed when I am still in depression myself God?"

He wanted me to go to the classes so that I could begin to heal. He wanted me to learn how I could eventually help others. He wanted me to look aro· and see all of the pain in one room. Many of us w sobbing from our trials and tribulations. Most of us wer still in the situations and depressed.

God told me, "You don't have any choice but to come out of your depression. If someone sees you depressed, you cannot help him or her. Everyone needs to let Me heal them and let Me use them."

I knew what God meant because the Bible says:

I Hate God

"And he spake a parable unto them, "Can the blind lead the blind? Shall they not both fall into the ditch?"
Luke 6:39 KJV

People need to see you conquer your emotions before you can help encourage them to deal with their pain. If they see you down and you tell them everything is going to be all right, then you are not leading by example.

Many times people give you bad advice. They mean well, but they have not walked in your shoes. Thus, I believe when we go through certain things in life; because of our deliverance, we can help others in that area.

I discovered that I had to face my pain. I could not keep getting angry with God. Being angry with God did not work. I decided no matter what, I was going to give God the glory. I continued to pray, fast, speak in tongues, and read the Word more than I ever did in my life. I was determine to conquer the situation regardless of the outcome. I decided to use my faith to be victorious. This time, I would not hate and be angry with God.

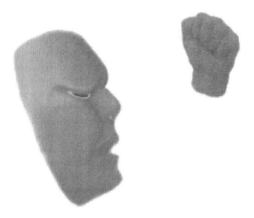

YOU HATE GOD

I was not living a God-fearing life during the years of 1983 to 1987. I was a backslider and I knew I was wrong. It is hard to live a life free from sin when you are lonely and desperate for someone to love you. Yes, I was desperate. I wanted comfort, love, and sex. It was wrong to commit fornication, but in my case, it was adultery. My first husband would not start the divorce proceedings and he avoided any paperwork that I sent. I kept sending him divorce documents through my lawyer repeatedly for about eight months. I decided to go ahead and live my life in spite of the situation.

My mother would call and tried to tell me about Jesus. I would put the phone down beside me without her knowing it because I did not want to hear what she had to say. She was making me feel guilty about my sinful life. Sometimes when she called, I would lie and tell her that I was too busy to talk. I was only watching television. Back then, I did not have caller ID. I would always answer the phone because it could have been my unit calling since I was in the army.

My mother was a praying woman. She knew that I was not going to church. She knew I was not praying to God about anything. I hurt my mother, but in my mind, she did not understand. My heart was hardened and I was rebellious.

Since God knew my mother could not reach me, He used other sources to get my attention. The first source He used was my children. God will use anyone. My children were five and four years old.

I was driving to the beach with my children. We lived less than five miles away from the beach so we went there all of the time. Thiess was sitting in the front seat and Bob J was sitting behind her.

Out of nowhere, my son said, "Mama."

I briefly turned and asked, "What?"

Bob J replied with concern, "You don't take us to church."

I abruptly said, "No, I don't."

He sternly asked, "Do you want to know what?"

I boldly probed, "What?"

He stared at me with piercing eyes and replied, "If Thiess and I go to Hell; it will be all your fault."

When I turned around to look at my son, he was pointing his finger at me. The guilt I felt was overwhelming. Nevertheless, that was not enough of a beat down to my spirit. Bob J starting singing as he looked out the car window, "Swing low, sweet chariot, coming to carry me home," and then Thiess joined him. They were bouncing their heads and I have no clue where they learned the words or tune to that song. I could not say anything because I was embarrassed and I was guilty as charged. I wanted to tell them to shut up, but I could not open my mouth to make them be quiet. I had to deal with it.

Immediately, I found them a church. The church had a community van, which picked-up and dropped-off my children. I would stay home because I was not ready to go to church. I was drinking, cussing, partying, and having a great time doing the things I wanted to do. Sin felt good. Living right meant I would not have comfort or an escape from reality. At the same token, I was not going to let my children make me feel guilty about their lives going to Hell. I made sure they went to church and it was a mistake.

What? How was it a mistake sending my children to church? Yes, it was a mistake. Apparently, the church was teaching that the prayer, 'Now I lay me down to sleep,' was a sin. I broke the prayer down and could not find a lie or a sinful act. I called and asked my mother. I called other Christians whom I knew. All of them agreed with me that I needed to remove my children from the church. This forced me to go to church sometimes. It was very uncomfortable. After a few months, I just could not go because it was too hard.

A few months later, I had guard duty for one week. We had a rotating shift around the clock. It was a cool day at Fort Ord, California. It was very difficult for me because I had to be away from Bob J and Thiess. The whole time that I was in the army was very rough for my children and me. My children were five and six years old and I was twenty-eight.

God showed up through two people while I was on guard duty. He sent both a Christian male soldier and a

Christian female soldier to talk to me. As I was walking by them, they were having Bible study. They stopped me and said that they needed to talk to me. I told them I had something to do. They assured me that they would not be long, so I went to see what they wanted.

The male soldier said, "God told me to tell you that He has something special He wants you to do, but you have to get right before you can do it."

The female soldier responded with a smile on her face, "That's what I was going to tell her. God also told me to give you these Bible verses."

I do not remember the Bible verses that she gave me; however, I remember the guilty feeling, which overpowered my spirit.

Feeling shameful, I asked, "What does God have special for me to do?"

He smiled and assured me, "I don't know, but God can't use you until you live right."

She shook her head and agreed, "Yeah, and it must be serious for both of us to have the same message. I did not talk to him about you. I thought he had something else to tell you."

He continued to say, "God will tell you what it is when you do as He asks."

The conversation took about two hours and I lost my time to eat or get a quick nap. I lost my time to make phone calls. I knew my mother was praying hard for God to come at me in every direction that I turned. Why wouldn't God just leave me alone and what was my special job?

I had to peel myself away from them. I could not take it anymore and replied, "Well, I got to go."

They both told me good-bye and they said we would

talk later.

A couple of weeks later, the same male soldier saw me and waved to get my attention. I walked up to him and he began to talk boldly to me.

He blatantly stated, "You hate God."

In shock, I became angry and sternly responded, "No, I don't."

He continued forcibly and insisting, "Yes, you do."

I became more irritated and countered, "No, I don't, that's a lie. I know that I am not living right at this moment in my life, but I don't hate God."

I did not realize it at the time, but God's spirit was swelling up in him and he confidently declared, "No, it isn't a lie. You hate God and you love Satan."

Now, I was really getting furious. How dare him to tell me such outlandish words.

I was upset and rebelled, "I am not listening to this anymore, I don't hate God and I don't love Satan."

He did not quit hammering me. He was persistent and equipped with the Word of God saying, "Yes, you do, I will show you."

He pulled out his Bible and turned to the scripture, which states:

"No man can serve two masters: for either he will hate the one, and love the other; or else he will hold to the one, and despise the other. Ye cannot serve God and mammon."
Matthew 6:24 KJV

He continued to tell me, "God told me to show you this. You are choosing to live in sin after God let you know that He has something special for you to do. This makes you hate God and love Satan. You cannot be in between. Either you will be for God or you won't."

This man was letting me know that there was no gray area with God. It was either white or black. I needed to get away from him. I could not take it anymore and I wanted him and God to leave me alone. I could not run and I could not hide. God was everywhere I went.

Feeling full of shame, I walked away saying, "Well, I got to go."

I heard him reply without me looking back, "I don't know why God keeps giving me messages to give you, but He must really want you to do something special. I love you and so does God."

For the next few weeks, that Bible verse bugged me. It was mind-boggling. I knew according to the scripture, I truly indeed hated God and loved Satan. I did not want to admit this. I did not want to accept it. I knew I had to change my life because God was hot on my trail and heavy on my spirit. I did not want to hate God. I was not making a conscious decision to hate Him. My actions dictated I hated God.

If you are a sinner, you hate God. The Word makes this crystal clear. Part of me did not want to change and the other part of me did want to transform my life. I decided to go back to the Lord; however, it would not be long before I would turn my back on God again because of fear.

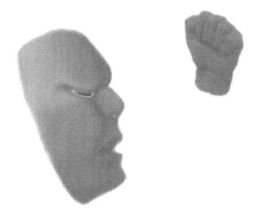

DEMONIC ATTACKS

Even though going to church was hard at first for me, my children were happy to be in the house of the Lord. Everything seemed to be going fine, but the enemy was not happy with the changes I made. I could not believe some of the things that I experienced really did exist. I did not believe in witchcraft or that the demons had any power; however, I only thought I had to fight temptations. I did not think people could put curses on you. I did not think demonic spirits could do anything to you. This is the hardest chapter for me to write since I still find these events to be unbelievable myself; however, this is my testimony. I am telling you the truth, these things actually happened to me. If you are going through some of these experiences, I have some advice that will help you to successfully overcome your attacks and find peace in God.

I was still in the army. Bob J and Thiess were six and

seven. Life was still difficult being a single mother in the military. I hated the army, but I was glad I had an income and I was good at my job.

Military families make a huge sacrifice for their country. From the spouses down to the children, this life is very tasking and demanding. After being a single parent in the armed forces, I applaud the single service members and the families who have both parents serving our nation.

I would have to say; God was the farthest thought on my mind. I did not go to church every Sunday, read the Bible, or pray. I was living a very dangerous life and did not even know it. When God was not present, I did not think about how I was living a life so full of risks. If I had died, it was very evident I was going to Hell. The Word states:

"I said therefore unto you, that ye shall die in your sins: for if ye believe not that I am he, ye shall die in your sins."
John 8:24 KJV

Since I came from a very strict home and the army was a very restricted job, I did not want to have more limitations in my life. I did not want God governing my actions through His Word or His Spirit. I did not want God to lead me. I just wanted to do Crisalyn. I did not realize that I was being my own god. Sin was freedom, but in reality, I was in bondage. It was invisible bondage, which was unseen to the carnal mind. I wanted sin. It felt good to party, commit fornication or adultery, cuss, and drink my alcohol. Sin was fun and it was freedom. Little did I know, I had shackles locking my destination to the Lake of Fire. My flesh controlled me more than the Holy Spirit.

If you are living in sin or committing iniquities over again as a saint, you are in bondage too and you being your own god. You need to correct your actions so that you will not end up in the Lake of Fire. The Bible says:

"For all have sinned, and come short of the glory of God:"
Romans 3:23 KJV

In addition to:

"Now the works of the flesh are manifest, which are these; adultery, fornication, uncleanness, lasciviousness, Idolatry, witchcraft, hatred, variance, emulations, wrath, strife, seditions, heresies,
Envyings, murders, drunkenness, revellings, and such like: of the which I tell you before, as I have also told you in time past, that they which do such things shall not inherit the kingdom of God."
Galatians 5:19-21 KJV

With that said, my life was in a treacherous mess. I was scared to die because I did not want to go to Hell; however, I was not afraid enough to change my life. I loved what I was doing. Changing was not in my atmosphere. I said all of this to set up the circumstances going on in my life during this period.

I sent my children to a babysitter who lived up the street. She had a friend who operated in witchcraft. One day the witch was at my babysitter's house. My children were there playing with both of their children. The witch was talking to the babysitter about witchcraft. My daughter overheard their conversation.

She looked at Thiess and said, "Do you believe in witches and witchcraft?"

Thiess replied, "No, we don't believe in that stuff."

Thiess was just six years old. I always questioned in my mind, why would this witch care if a six-year-old believed in witchcraft or not? Why didn't she talk to me about this instead of my child?

The witch evilly told my daughter, "Well, you will believe, just wait until you see what will happen to you, your brother, and your mother tomorrow morning."

Thiess unbelievingly responded, "Okay."

My daughter did not know what to do. She did not know whether to be scared or not. Thiess did not mention this to me at all when she came home that day.

The next morning, I combed my daughter's hair. Lo and behold, there were bugs all over in her hair. It was packed and loaded with lice and eggs.

I was shocked and confused while saying, "Where did these bugs come from, they weren't here yesterday?"

Bob J and Thiess responded at the same time, "I don't know."

Sounding concern I said, "Bob J, come here and let me see if you have lice in your hair."

To my surprise, lice was in my son's hair. I decided to look in the mirror at my hair and I had them.

All of our faces revealed disbelief. I could not go to work. All three of us had to go to the hospital. It was that serious.

The military doctor was stunned. He assumed what was not. He asked, "Wow, don't you guys comb your hair every day? It is impossible for you to get this many lice and their eggs overnight."

I insisted with sincerity, "I am telling you, sir, I comb our hair every day and there was nothing in our hair yesterday."

I could tell he did not believe me. The impossible happened. He gave us some medication to wash our hair. He also gave us something to put in our heads to kill the eggs. We could not go anywhere for a few days. Thiess and my hair was long flowing down our backs. I made the command decision to cut our hair. Both of us were saddened and cried; however, we did not want the lice in our hair. After I made sure, all of the good-for-nothing-bugs were out of all of our heads, we returned to our regular routines.

When my children went back to the babysitter's, that afternoon the witch came over to see her. Apparently, that was not the only person she wanted to see. She wanted to see Thiess.

The witch questioned my daughter, "Did anything happen to you, your brother, and your mother?"

Thiess was puzzled and probed, "What do you mean?"

The witch asked her with an uninviting smile, "Did you guys get some lice in your heads?"

Thiess became scared. She frightfully said, "Yes, how did you know?"

The witch responded wickedly, "I am the one that summoned that curse on you guys. Now do you believe I am a witch and do you believe in witchcraft?"

Thiess was so terrified; she replied, "Yes."

My daughter could not wait for me to come home from work. She was too nervous to tell her brother. This was a very long day for Thiess. The witch kept smiling at her on and off while she was there. My daughter did not know what to do. When I came home from work, I picked up my children.

My daughter was too petrified to talk about her afternoon. At the same time, she was too afraid to keep this to herself. Thiess slowly said, "Mom, I need to tell you something."

I was curious and asked, "What do you need to tell me?"

The fear in her face showed everything. She reluctantly began to explain, "The lady that lives across the street from the babysitter told me that she is a witch and she caused those lice to be in our heads."

I replied adamantly, "I don't believe in witches and witchcraft."

Thiess innocently said, "That's what I told her the day before the bugs were in our heads."

My daughter proceeded to tell me the whole story. I immediately called my mother because this concerned me. She listened quietly until I finished.

With uncertainty, I posed the question and asked, "Mom, witches and witchcraft don't exist, do they? I can't believe it."

She replied with a sigh, "I am afraid so Crissy. You need to get you another babysitter. Get as far away from them as you can. It is in the Bible about witches and witchcraft. You see, the devil has power too, and he has followers."

The Bible says:

"There shall not be found among you any one that maketh his son or his daughter to pass through the fire, or that useth divination, or an observer of times, or an

enchanter, or a witch,
Or a charmer, or a consulter with familiar spirits, or a
wizard, or a necromancer.
For all that do these things are an abomination unto the
Lord: and because of these abominations the Lord thy
God doth drive them out from before thee."
Deuteronomy 18:10-12 KJV

If witchcraft does not exist, then why does the Bible mention it several times? There are even examples of witchcraft and sorcery in the Bible. Here is an instance where a witch raised Samuel the prophet from the grave for King Saul.

"Then said Saul unto his servants, Seek me a woman that hath familiar spirit, that I may go to her, and inquire of her. And his servants said to him, Behold, there is a woman that hath a familiar spirit at Endor. And Saul disguised himself, and put on other raiment, and he went, and two men with him, and they came to the woman by night: and he said, I pray thee, divine unto me by the familiar spirit, and bring me him up whom I shall name unto thee. And the woman said unto him, Behold, thou knowest what Saul has done, how he hath cut off those that have familiar spirits, and the wizards, out of the land: wherefore then layest thou a snare for my life, to cause me to die?
And Saul sware to her by the Lord saying, As the Lord liveth, there shall no punishment happen to thee for this thing. Then said the woman, Whom shall I bring up unto thee? And he said, Bring me up Samuel. And when the woman saw Samuel, she cried with a loud voice: and the woman spake to Saul, saying, Why hast thou deceived

me? For thou art Saul and the king said unto her, What form is he of? And she said, An old man cometh up; and he is covered with a mantle. And Saul perceived that it was Samuel, and he stooped with his face to the ground, and bowed himself."
1 Samuel 28:7-14 KJV

This shows an example of witchcraft. When Samuel was disturbed from his death, he was not pleased that Saul had summoned him. He told Saul that his sons and he would be joining him in death for his action. There are consequences for practicing witchcraft. The Bible says:

"Because thou obeyedst not the voice of the Lord, nor executedst his fierce wrath upon Amalek, therefore hath the Lord done this thing unto this day.
Moreover the Lord will also deliver Israel with thee into the hand of the Philistines: and tomorrow shalt thou and thy sons be with me: the Lord also shall deliver the host of Israel into the hand of the Philistines."
1 Samuel 28:18-19 KJV

I was stunned because this was the first time I ever heard my mother talking about this subject. She never showed me this information in the Word. I thought with all of her teachings, I knew everything there was about the Bible and what was in the Bible. I never knew Satan had power either because I only thought he could only tempt you. This revelation still did not prepare me for what I was about to face. Now for the first time, I was scared. Thiess was not the only one who was frightened. As a mother, I had to encourage her that we would be fine. I did not know what else to do. I did as my mother instructed me concerning the babysitter. I found another sitter and I tried not to go see the people down the street as much as possible.

As time went by, I knew I needed to return to church. As I reflect on my past, I needed a spirit-filled church. I knew God was not going to keep His hand of protection on me as long as I was living in sin. My mother's prayers covered me. This was not enough since I was at the age of accountability. If Satan had power, I knew I was not a match for him. The only way to have a fighting chance was to give my life back to the Lord.

I found a church to go to in Seaside, California. Everything went fine for a few weeks. I was getting stronger spiritually, but I was still very weak. I had a lot to learn because I did not know enough about God. The Word says:

"My people are destroyed for lack of knowledge: because thou hast rejected knowledge, I will also reject thee, that thou shalt be no priest to me: seeing thou hast forgotten the law of thy God, I will also forget thy children."
Hosea 4:6 KJV

One evening in my living room, I decided to teach my children some Bible stories. They were sitting on the floor looking up at me. I had the Bible on my lap and I began to read it to them. While I was reading the Word, some dishes fell out of the cabinet in the kitchen. Please note there was no storms, earthquake, or any one physically standing in the kitchen to explain why the dishes fell out of the cabinet. We were so terrified. I immediately shut my Bible.

I looked up to God and prayed, "God, if you want me to go to church and read Your Word, You are going to have to send me a husband to deal with this."

Bob J asked me, "What's going on, Mom?"

Assuring my son, all I knew to say was, "I don't know, but we are not going to worry about it."

I had to show them that I was not scared when in reality I needed someone to comfort and protect me. As their mother, I had to make them feel safe even when I did not think our surroundings were harmless.

A few days later, I tried to read the Bible alone to see if anything would happen and it did. I had an item on the piano. It popped off and fell on the floor. Again, I shut the Bible.

That night when I went to bed, something happened more frightening. I went to bed to go to sleep. Suddenly, I was in a paralyzed state from head to toe. I tried to move my body; however, it was hopeless. This time was different from when I was in college. I felt an evil presence in and around my body. I had tremendous fear. I thought I was going to die. I could not scream, talk, or move. I did not know what to do because I could not do anything. My body began to lift off the bed. After being in a levitated state over my bed for a few seconds, I finally dropped on the bed. It released me and I was able to move. I immediately sat up and did not go to sleep for hours that night. I was crying because I was alone and I believed no one could help or save me. This experience terrified me. At least once or twice a week this became an unwanted occurrence.

One time, I took a sleeping pill. Unbelievably, this did not stop anything either, and the result was the same.

My paralyzed body continued to haunt me. Sometimes it would levitate over the bed. Sometimes the wind would gush in one ear and out the other ear, and sometimes there would be a foul smell.

I was in so much fear that I went back to talk to the Christian female soldier. I told her about all of the happenings which I had endured.

She claimed with conviction, "The devil is a liar. I am going to have some of my church prayer warriors come over to your house Sunday. These women have God's anointing on their lives. We will pray and anoint your home with oil."

I told her with resistance and hesitation, "No, that's okay. I just needed to talk. Don't worry about it, I will be alright."

She refused to listen to my wishes. She boldly replied, "I will see you Sunday. We are coming anyway, so be expecting us."

My first thought was, do not be at home, but deep inside I wanted these experiences to end. At the spark of hope, I was home when they arrived. You could tell these women were very spiritual. They did not ask me if they could go ahead and pray. They pulled out their praying oil and began to anoint my house. They cast out demons in every room. They bound the enemy. Finally, they told us to hold hands with them so that they could pray for us. Thiess was on my left and Bob J was on my right. We bowed our heads as the prayer warrior began to pray. While we were praying, something felt strange about my son. I opened my eyes and Bob J looked like he was beholding something in the heavens. I closed my eyes for the rest of the prayer.

One of the prayer warriors gave me the most

powerful words to use if I had any more demonic attacks. Those words I still use to this day.

You could tell she operated in power and lived a holy life with the Lord. She was fierce with her prayer. She stood her ground with the enemy and then she gave me these instructions, "Now this is what I want you to do if you ever have any more of these satanic attacks. I want you to plead the blood of Jesus. You say I bind you in the name of Jesus and His precious blood. Say this with authority. You cannot say it, as if you do not mean it or believe it. You have to put your foot down as if you were disciplining your children. The devil is beneath your feet. This means we as believers have authority over him. There is power in the name of Jesus. Satan will have to flee."

The prayer warrior gave me the following Bible verses:

"And the God of peace shall bruise Satan under your feet shortly. The grace of our Lord Jesus Christ be with you. Amen."
Romans 16:20 KJV

In addition, she gave me:

"Ye are of God, little children, and have overcome them: because greater is he that is in you, than he that is in the world."
1 John 4:4 KJV

I did not want them to leave. I still feared the unknown. All I said to her was, "Okay."

This event affected me so much, that it started my

spiritual growth. The lesson I learned was I could overpower the enemy for the rest of my life. I still had a long way to go; however, this was the beginning of my spiritual warfare against demonic attacks. I will admit; I was hoping that I would never have to use those words. I was hoping that the prayer warriors took care of the problem. Unfortunately, it did not solve the issues. For now, I had to find out what did my son see when he looked up into the heavens. After they left, I called my son and he responded.

"Bob J," I asked, "did you see something when those ladies were praying?"

His face still looked flushed as he replied, "Yes, ma'am." He was being very careful.

I curiously probed, "What did you see?"

Bob J was very descriptive and responded, "I saw a man with white wool hair and fire in his eyes."

Not sure if he knew what he was saying I questioned him gently, "Wow, do you know who you saw?"

With uncertainty in his voice Bob J replied, "An angel or something?"

I told him with a smile in my heart and on my face, "You saw Jesus. That is how the Bible describes Him."

I had never told my son about the description of Jesus in the book of Revelation. It says:

"His head and his hairs were white like wool, as white as snow; and his eyes were as a flame of fire;" Revelation 1:14 KJV

I knew for sure and without a doubt, God was there with us. I still feared what was about to come after the prayer warriors prayed. Knowing the Lord allowed my son to see Jesus made a difference. I knew that scripture because Revelation was and still is my favorite book of the Bible. This book scared me straight. When I went to bed, for the first time in months, I had some peace. This did not last for a lengthy period because the enemy came back and I had to use the words I was taught.

When I had gotten comfortable, I began to let my guard down. The demonic attacks had not happened in a few weeks. Caught by surprise, they began again. Paralyzed as soon as I stretched out on my bed with my head on the pillow, I was frightened. I remembered what the prayer warrior instructed me to do. Since I could not talk, I began to demand my release with my mind.

I commanded with authority, "In the name of Jesus and His blood, I demand you set me free."

I could not speak this aloud. It did not let me go at first, so I said it with more of a commanding force in my head.

With all of my faith, I had at the time, I repeated and said, "I said in the name of Jesus and His precious blood I demand you set me free."

The Word says:

"And Jesus said unto them, Because of your unbelief: for verily I say unto you, If ye have faith as a grain of mustard seed, ye shall say unto this mountain, Remove hence to yonder place; and it shall remove; and nothing shall be impossible unto you."
Matthew 17:20 KJV

God had given me those words through his servant. I had to believe this no matter what level of faith I had. It released me immediately. This was the first time the demonic forces freed me because I used the power of Jesus' name and His blood. My fear of this evil force began to leave. It was a spiritual battle, but I began to gain control. The Bibles says:

"And the seventy returned again with joy, saying, Lord, even the devils are subject unto us through thy name. And he said unto them, I beheld Satan as lightning fall from heaven.
Behold, I give unto you power to tread on serpents and scorpions, and over all the power of the enemy: and nothing shall by any means hurt you."
Luke 10:17-19 KJV

You have the power to take control over the enemy. Once you realize this, you can begin to free yourself with the power of God. If you are not serving God because you fear attacks from demonic forces, know that God is more powerful. He will help you to be victorious over the demonic forces. These attacks may increase at first, but eventually they will end. You need to fast and pray. It is not always enough to state the Word. The Bible says:

"And he said unto them, This kind can come forth by nothing, but by prayer and fasting."
Mark 9:29 KJV

A few years later, I remarried. My duty assignment was in Germany. I am a rape victim. One night, I woke up with a dark black demonic spirit was on top of me having a good time, I cannot explain how this made me feel. I tried not to talk about this experience to this day.

My husband at the time was lying next to me asleep. Since I could not scream because of my paralyzed state, I began to plead the blood of Jesus. This demon hit me to shut me up and continued doing what he was doing. I was shocked because this was the first time any of them hit me let alone touch me in that manner. This was a stronger force. This demon resisted hearing the blood of Jesus. It was a good thing that I was stronger with God spiritually. I continued to plead the blood of Jesus louder in my mind more forcefully. At this time, I learned how to declare and decree God's Word.

Even in my fear, I insisted repeatedly, "I demand, command, and declare in the name of Jesus' blood that you set me free."

Finally, it set me free. The demon grunted as he freed me. This let me know he was angry. I immediately prayed to God.

This experience humbled me and enlightened me that I was still vulnerable. I began to pray, "God, please never let a demonic spirit touch me again. My body is Your temple, Lord. Thank you for freeing me God. In Jesus' name, Amen."

The Bible says:

"What? Know ye not that your body is the temple of the Holy Ghost which is in you, which ye have of God, and ye are not your own?
For ye are bought with a price: therefore glorify God in your body, and in your spirit, which are God's."
1 Corinthians 6:19-20 KJV

This has never happened to me again because God honored my prayer. I had reminded God that my body was His temple. I now rarely go through these demonic attacks. I overpowered them with the blood of Jesus. It works every time. The prayer warrior gave me some powerful tools and currently I use all of my spiritual weapons. These needed words were effective then as they are still operational today. Let the power of Jesus' blood be a resource in your life. He will do wonders for anyone who will use His Word. The Word says:

"For there is no respect of persons with God."
Romans 2:11 KJV

Just as God gave me the words to stop these demonic attacks, He has now given them to you. Do not be afraid because Satan and his fallen angels have limited powers. They are not as powerful as the Almighty God. Without God, you do not have any power. When you accept God in your life, you have more power than your enemy does.

God also gave me a huge revelation. When Lucifer raged a war in the heavens, the archangel Michael only said one thing. He said, *"The Lord rebuke thee."* The battle ended. The Word says:

"Yet Michael the archangel, when contending with the devil he disputed about the body of Moses, durst not bring against him a railing accusation, but said, The Lord rebuke thee."
Jude 1:9 KJV

Michael is a very powerful angel. Angels are more powerful than we are. If Michael is saying the Lord rebuke you, then we need to say the Lord rebuke you. I am amazed what these words are doing. The devil is defeated when we apply specific scriptures to our situations and use all of the weapons God has given us. The demonic forces cannot keep you in bondage. Our God created us all. None of His creations can overpower God collectively or individually. This means that if anything attacks you, whether it is witchcraft or demonic, these satanic sources cannot overpower you if you use the knowledge given to you in the Word of God.

Demonic attacks are scare tactics that the enemy uses while convincing you to remain living a sinful life. This means, you will continue to hate God. Be strong and fight the good fight of faith. Show the enemy that he is the one whom you hate because you are now serving the Lord and you will love God for the rest of your days.

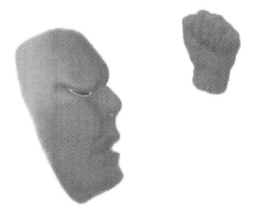

SEVENTEEN YEARS

I was talking on the phone with my father one day. During this time of my life, I was becoming stronger in the Lord. I was going to church and I was living right to the best of my ability. I knew God enough to recognize His miracles and visions. I knew God communicated with His people in unique ways and through different people. On this day, God was about to show my father and me the miracles that He did for us. My father was no longer in prison and he was on probation. The following conversation shocked both of us.

My father was happy to hear from me and said, "I was thinking about calling you, but you beat me to it."

While I was laughing, I answered, "Wow, we are thinking about each other at the same time."

As the conversation progressed, my father proceeded to tell me something that he had never told me. He spoke in detail about the letter he had written to God in prison. I was amazed at his story. Finally, I was able to solve the puzzle.

I was flabbergasted and replied with my new revelation, "What? Dad, you are not going to believe this." I proceeded to tell my father about my visions and the inner body episodes at Ohio State.

My father was astounded and said, "Wow, I did not know you went through that."

Neither one of us had told the other about our experiences until that day. Realizing that it was the power of God, I said, "Dad, those were miracles. God did those miracles in our lives. He answered your prayer. Wow, those were actually visions. I did not know because I was not serving God during that time. It was an act of God controlling my body. We are walking miracles Dad. Our lives are living testimonies. What a revelation. To God be the glory, I am tripping."

My father was shocked and said, "Wow, I am tripping too Daughter. Well, I knew God was mad at me when the tornado came. I will never do that again."

With a firm, respectful tone, I replied, "Yeah, Dad, don't ever do that again; you might not get to live through it the next time."

My father assured me, "You got that right."

Finally, having closure, I told him, "Man, I thought I was losing my mind. I did not understand what was going on with me."

My father reemphasized, "Well, now you know you weren't crazy and I know I wasn't crazy either."

In disbelief, I asked, "Wow, how many years did it take for us to tell each other our testimonies?"

My father responded, "I don't know."

My curiosity was high and I had to know. I said, "Let

me figure this out."

Since I love math, I began to calculate how many years it had been.

With excitement, I reported, "Dad, it took seventeen years for us to talk about this. Now, everything makes sense."

He questioned with inquisitiveness, "Do you want to know what doesn't make any sense?"

Not knowing what my father was going to say, I probed, "What?"

He said with a joking voice, "The tornado leveled some of the buildings across the street, but it did not touch one brick on the penitentiary. Why?"

We roared laughing.

He continued to say while laughing, "Since God leveled the other buildings; He could have leveled the pen so that we all could escape. So I became angrier seeing every brick intact. This made me hate God even more than I already did, to tell you the truth."

As we continued talking, I said, "Well, Dad, I just thanked God for the lesson He gave you."

He laughed, "Yeah, the lesson was, none of you prisoners are coming out of here."

Chuckling and joking with my father was fun. So I added while emphasizing the word 'world', "Dad, if that had of happened, Atlanta wouldn't have been in trouble, the world would have been in trouble."

We continued to laugh. We were both still in shock how God's timing and intervention were a part of both of our lives. He orchestrated the whole thing. What a mighty God we serve. This was proof to me that God is the same today, yesterday, and forever more. He is the same God who created us, parted the Red Sea, appeared in a burning bush, saved Daniel in the lion's den, and the other many marvelous miracles, which we read in the Bible.

Pleading with my father, "Please Dad, don't ever talk to God like that again. You got away with it the first time, but I don't think you will be able to push your luck doing that again."

Joking, he replied, "No Daughter, I won't ever do that again, I promise. Do you want to know why?"

I knew my father had something crazy to say. He is a natural, undiscovered comedian. He is so talented and can make a joke out of anything on the spot.

Laughing, while catching my breath, "Why Dad?"

"Because I want to go to Heaven so that I can steal all of the gold up there."

Shocked, I stuttered, "What? You… cannot steal all of the gold in Heaven. There's way too much for you to carry or handle."

Assuring me, "I am sure enough going to try."

By this time, our laughter was out of control. My father had gone mad.

Catching my breath, "Dad, the streets are made of gold. How in the world are you going to steal that?"

After he gathered his thoughts he slowly replied, "I will figure that out when I get there. A thief always cases out the area first."

I could not believe my ears. My father was talking so much trash and I lost my composure.

"Not that I am trying to help you Dad, but did you know that the gold on earth is not as shiny as the gold in Heaven?"

"That's all the more reason I need to steal it Daughter. I want all of it. I will never be broke again."

Laughing even harder, neither one of us could talk for a minute. I was through with my father.

"But Dad, there will be plenty of gold for everyone. God will have all the gold you want and need. There won't be any reason to steal when you get to Heaven."

"Daughter, haven't you heard... once a thief, always a thief. When I get to Heaven, I am going to steal all of the gold up there since I couldn't steal it all down here."

"Dad, you are a mess. Nevertheless, I guess you are my mess. You are missing your calling. You should be on stage somewhere with all of the jokes you have."

Calmly, he laughed, "This time it's not a joke... Do you know why I want all of the gold in Heaven?"

"No, sir."

He sighed with a deep breath, "Because deep down in my heart, I feel it's all mine."

Both of us just laughed so hard to the point it was ridiculous.

Then I questioned him, "If it is not a joke Dad, then why are we laughing."

"I don't know, why don't you tell me."

We continued to enjoy the rest of our conversation. I hung up the phone in disbelief. God had controlled my body with accuracy for a couple of hours in my life to find my father. This was unbelievable. Now, my father and I are able to tell jokes about life and Heaven. We came a long way.

God gave us a chance to decide whether we would worship Him. Please don't make the wrong decision. You are responsible for any wrong choices and you will suffer the consequences. The Bible says:

"For the wages of sin is death; but the gift of God is

I Hate God

eternal life through Jesus Christ our Lord."
Romans 6:23 KJV

There is a price to pay for your sins. There are rewards for worshipping and serving God. You have to choose your path. The Word states:

"And if it seem evil unto you to serve the Lord, choose you this day whom ye will serve; whether the gods which your fathers served that were on the other side of the flood, or the gods of the Amorites, in whose land ye dwell: but as for me and my house, we will serve the Lord."
Joshua 24:15 KJV

It also states:

"If any man will do his will, he shall know of the doctrine, whether it be of God, or whether I speak of myself."
John 7:17

You have freewill. Choose your decision wisely, because the consequences or the rewards are going to be for eternity. The Word also says:

"But the fearful, and unbelieving, and the abominable, and murderers, and whoremongers, and sorcerers, and idolaters, and all liars, shall have their part in the lake which burneth with fire and brimstone: which is the second death."
Revelations 21:8 KJV

I came to this conclusion; I have already lived Hell on earth. A lot of my life has been unbearable from a broken heart several times, physical pain from abuse, sickness, and surgeries. I have lived in fear of demonic activities. I do not want to go to a worse place, which will burn at higher temperatures than the hottest country in the world.

If you go to Hell, it is by your own freewill. You are volunteering by your choices you are living today. You must keep in mind; God made Hell for the fallen angels. The Word says:

"Then shall he say also unto them on the left hand, Depart from me, ye cursed, into everlasting fire, prepared for the devil and his angels:"
Matthew 25:41 KJV

The two highest creations made by God were the angels and humankind. God created the planets, stars, moon, sun, trees, flowers, and animals. None of these creations has ever rebelled against God. Only God's two highest creations rebelled against Him. Why is that? The angels who are now fallen angels only had one time to rebel. For some reason, God has mercy on man. He sacrificed His only begotten Son's blood ensuring that man had every opportunity to receive salvation. You do not want to go to a place made for these fallen angels. Don't take your salvation for granted. Man could have been given only one chance to mess up too if God chose the same fate for us.

If you do not believe God exists, ask God to prove Himself to you. As you saw, God showed Himself to a sinner in prison who actually hated Him. God will prove

He exists for you too, if you just ask Him. You do not have to do something as far-fetched as my father did for God to prove who He is. All you have to do is make your request known to Him.

My brother Anthony asked God when he was a teenager, "God, if you exist, I want to find five dollars on the ground today. This will let me know you are real."

Do you want to know what? My brother found a five-dollar bill that day. Ever since then, my brother believed God existed whether he was living right or not. This is all you have to do. Ask God with respect. He will hear and answer you. I have shown you two examples of God proving His existence. It is up to you to use your faith to believe in God. It is up to you to choose the right choice of hating or loving God. What is your final choice?

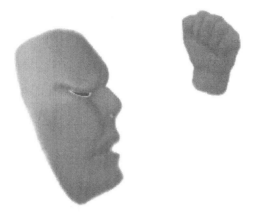

CONQUERED

I was alone while my son went off to war to Afghanistan. Even though I was lonely, the new surroundings were not as painful as the one I had to leave. I could see and experience things, which I had never seen or done before in my life. I did not have to experience snow, especially since I hate snow. I did not have to take chances of seeing the husband who rejected and hurt me. I did not have to face the man who broke my heart into countless pieces. I did not have to see people who would question me. I did not have to live where I was not wanted. Most of all, I did not want to face the reality that my life fell apart again right before my eyes. I could not control anything that was happening in my life.

At first, living alone in a new state and city, while being depressed, did very little to help me. However, I did feel better knowing I had moved far away from my painful surroundings. Many days, I poured out my tears before the Lord all day. My eyes were bloodshot red. The torment on my face showed great despair. My spirit left nothing inside of me. I was completely weary and drained from all of life itself. My heart was broken beyond repair. But God... but God.

The Lord began to work with me. He told me things to read in the Bible. I was surprised at the information that I did not know. The Bible says:

"My brethren, count it all joy when ye fall into divers temptations."
James 1:2 KJV

I did not understand this verse in the beginning. I read other translations. These translations said temptations were temptations, trials, troubles, and tests. I could now see the meaning of this Bible verse. God wanted me to live *James 1:2*. How was I supposed to do this? I did not feel any joy in the midst of my pain. God gave me a second verse. It says:

"Blessed is the man that endureth temptation: for when he is tried, he shall receive the crown of life, which the Lord hath promised to them that love him."
James 1:12 KJV

Furthermore, it says:

"Blessed are they which are persecuted for righteousness' sake: for theirs is the kingdom of heaven. Blessed are ye, when men shall revile you, and persecute you, and shall say all manner of evil against you falsely,

for my sake.
Rejoice, and be exceeding glad: for great is your reward in heaven: for so persecuted they the prophets which were before you."
Matthew 5:10-12 KJV

This let me know, the more that I suffered, the greater would be my reward in Heaven. I began to get strength to become strong enough to endure the pain face-to-face. From there, I began to conquer every dart thrown at me by the enemy. My prayers became stronger and I was able to live again without feeling sorry for myself.

I began to break witchcraft out of my life. I began to fight for my deliverance. The more I fought, the more they fought. They forgot one thing; I had the power of the Almighty God on my side.

During this time, I read the entire Bible for the first time. I discovered; I was lacking knowledge and there were scriptures that I did not understand. The Bible says:

"My people are destroyed for the lack of knowledge: because thou hast rejected knowledge, I will also reject thee, that thou shalt be no priest to me: seeing thou hast forgotten the law of thy God, I will also forget thy children. "
Hosea 4:6 KJV

I began to use God's words of power. I knew I could bind the enemy, but I did not know to *loose* the opposite of whatever I bind. The Word says:

101

"Verily I say unto you, "Whatsoever ye shall bind on earth shall be bound in heaven: and whatsoever ye shall loose on earth shall be loosed in heaven."
Matthew 18:18 KJV

I knew I had to change my thoughts, heart, and increase my knowledge in order to conquer the enemy. I was at war, whether I wanted to be or not and I had to face the battle. I prayed for understanding of the scriptures and studied them. I had to put on the full armor of God and begin to fight the battle in the middle of my depression.

"Put on the whole armor of God, that ye may be able to stand against the wiles of the devil."
Ephesians 6:11 KJV

My depression was my weakest link. There was no time to stay in this emotional state. I had to focus on winning this war. I would study how to fight witchcraft. They cannot have power over you with their curses if you are in tune with God. The more they fought me, the closer I drew to God. My faith began to grow. I had to be the conqueror because I was not going to let the Lord look weak in my life. This was an unwelcome fight, but I had to fight it.

At the same time, demons were trying to attack me. They wanted me to stop pleading the blood of Jesus against them. One female demon appeared before me and wanted me to leave everything alone so that she could have dominion over my situation. I refused. This female spirit of seduction had taken away my marriage. I was not about to let go of my Heavenly Father or my salvation. This was all I had left. God says in His Word:

"And he said, Hearken ye, all Judah, and ye inhabitants of Jerusalem, and thou king Jehoshaphat, Thus saith the Lord unto you, Be not afraid nor dismayed by reason of this great multitude; for the battle is not yours, but God's."
2 Chronicles 20:15 KJV

Moreover, it says:

"For we wrestle not against flesh and blood, but against principalities, against powers, against the rulers of the darkness of this world, against spiritual wickedness in high places."
Ephesians 6:12 KJV

This told me, without God, I was not going to get out of depression or overpower my enemies. I could not fight what I could not see. I could not see my emotions. I could not see my enemies. I was fighting a spiritual war. I continued studying the Word of God. The Lord revealed all of my enemies to me. I was shocked to find out some of my enemies were people who are close to me and in my family. This deeply hurt my heart and it took me weeks to recover from this devastating blow. The Word says:

"Now the works of the flesh are manifest, which are these; adultery, fornication uncleanness, lasciviousness, Idolatry, witchcraft, hatred, variance, emulations, wrath, strife, seditions, heresies, envyings, murders, drunkenness, revellings, and such like: of the which I

tell you before, as I have also told you in time past, that they which do such things shall not inherit the kingdom of God."
Galatians 5:19-21 KJV

I prayed for the strength to fight this battle. It was a battle that I did not want to combat. I just wanted to heal from my depression. I did not want to take on spiritual wars. To make matters worse, I had to fight sickness in my body. During this time, I had a mini stroke. To this day, I still feel some numbness in my body. I was praising the Lord, when it happened. My body popped inside, but I refused to stop praising God. The stroke left numbness at the bottom of my right foot under my toes and the tip of my right thumb. How ironic. Look at what the Word of God says about thumbs and toes.

But Adonibezek fled; and they pursued after him, and caught him, and cut off his thumbs and his great toes.
And Adonibezek said, Threescore and ten kings, having their thumbs and their great toes cut off, gathered their meat under my table: as I have done, so God hath requited me. And they brought him to Jerusalem, and there he died."
Judges 1:6-7 KJV

There are more Bible verses about thumbs and toes. If you cut off your thumbs and toes, it is hard to do normal functions such as picking things up or walking. It is humiliating. It weakens the ability to perform simple tasks and maneuvering from place to place.

Part of my body was weak. The attacks would not stop. I thought I was going to die from many of my attacks. I grew weary, and I welcomed death because there were too many battles to fight at one time. I was overwhelmed and I cried out to the Lord constantly for His help. The Word says:

"I will lift up mine eyes unto the hills, from whence cometh my help.
My help cometh from the Lord, which made heaven and earth."
Psalm 121:1-2 KJV

I had to believe this. I did believe this. It was the only way to conquer all of the enemies' attacks. I desired to find peace. It was my time to become stronger spiritually. There was no way around it. I had to go through the trial and face all of the battles.

All of my answers were in the Bible. I read things that I had never heard. I knew I was on the right track because when I tried to read the Word, I would fall asleep. I had to pray against the sleeping spirit.

I prayed, "God, please don't let me fall asleep when I read Your Word. I need to be stronger and the only way to do this is to learn Your instructions. Thank you God for keeping me awake and for Your strength. In Jesus' name, amen."

Eventually, I did not fall asleep when I read the Bible. I had to choose to stay focused and win this battle no matter how long it took. This fight did not leave overnight. It did not leave in days or months. This battle has been well over three years now, but I am winning. God is victorious and He does not lose. It may look like I lost, but God has held me. He has molded me. Most of all, I am not depressed. Yes, I still hurt from what people have done to me, but I learned to have the joy of the Lord in the midst of my tribulations.

No one can overpower the God in me. They might knock me down, but I will get back up and fight some more in the spirit. I accept the challenge. I have the most powerful Being on my side, which is God. No demon, witch, or man can defeat me as long as I let God have the steering wheel. I have to trust Him just as the Word says to do.

"Trust in the Lord with all thine heart; and lean not unto thine own understanding.
In all thy ways acknowledge him, and he shall direct thy paths."
Proverbs 3:5-6 KJV

I failed the tests in my past, but I have succeeded this time. I still have to control my thoughts and think positive. I refuse to let life get the best of me. The more I fight the enemy, the stronger I become. People tell me they can see the change in my life and now, I must agree. I am not the same person whom I was in 2011 on Thanksgiving Day when my husband whom I loved dearly told me that I was not wanted or loved. My whole world as I knew it turned upside down and changed.

Despite of whatever pain you feel, concentrate on God. I am focused on God's will, verses my sorrow. You can't tell by my appearance that I am battling anything. God has me covered. I have given the situation totally to God and this is where it will stay. I do not need to worry myself with a war already won by Him. I need to concentrate on helping others and get to the glorious kingdom of Heaven. I do not have time to be concerned with the evil doings of others.

I have to forgive them and move on with my life. I have to be obedient to God. He has much work for me to do. When I do this, then God will protect me as I go from one spiritual battle to another battle. When I feel the enemy's attacks now, I just say, "The Lord rebukes you."

Do you know how powerful those words are? Use these words when the enemy attacks. These words have transformed me and they will change you. They are conquering words. These words are in the Bible. It says:

"And the Lord said unto Satan, The Lord rebuke thee, O Satan; even the Lord that hath chosen Jerusalem rebuke thee: is not this a brand plucked out of the fire?"
Zechariah 3:2 KJV

Let me clarify this point, I used to say, "I rebuke you." I came to realize that there was something more powerful I needed to say which is, "The Lord rebukes you," because Satan only obeys God's Word. When I say this, the results are much faster. The most High God has the situation under control while He strips all of the demonic forces' power. I came out of the circumstances completely giving all the glory to God. Since Satan respects the Word of God, he obeys the Lord's commands. The Bible also says:

"And the evil spirit answered and said, Jesus I know, and Paul I know; but who are ye?
And the man in whom the evil spirit was leaped on them, and overcame them, and prevailed against them, so that they fled out of that house naked and wounded."

I Hate God

Acts 19:15-16 KJV

No demon, witch, or Satan himself can overpower the Lord. They cannot overpower the name of Jesus or His blood. The demonic forces know the name of Jesus and His followers. They know who you are if you serve God. If you don't serve God, the enemy can defeat you. Prayer, fasting, faith, love, and forgiveness, are also stronger than the enemy is and you have to know this. I learned these things from my studies and as God revealed them to me.

If I had taken this same path in my past, I would not have shown God hate. I did not want to disappoint Him again because He does more for me than the destroyer. God was not going to let me lose the war this time. I was now the conqueror because of the fact Jesus is in my life. He died on the cross for all of our sickness, hurt, pain, sins, trials, tribulations, and failures over two thousand years ago. I was not going to let our Savior do this in vain. I surrendered everything and gave my situations over to Him. When He rose from the grave, at that very moment, we received victory. Through Jesus Christ, I had conquered the enemy. I learned to make my faith show with my actions. The Word says:

"But without faith it is impossible to please him: for he that cometh to God must believe that he is, and that he is a rewarder of them that diligently seek him."
Hebrews 11:6 KJV

You will need to exercise faith too if you want to please God. It takes faith to know that the Lord exists. I knew that there was a God even as a sinner. I decided that it was time to demonstrate my faith and love for God, instead of displaying that I hated Him. It is also time for you to stop hating God if your life is not reflecting love for the Heavenly Father.

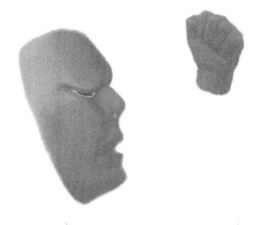

LAND OF GOD HATERS

I remember my first day of Kindergarten. The teacher announced herself and we had to introduce ourselves. She told us the rules that we had to follow. She told us how we would start the day. Our day would start with prayer and then we would say the 'Pledge of Allegiance.' This went on for many years until about the seventh or eighth grade. Why did it stop? It stopped because we had entered into the land of God haters.

I studied some of the history concerning this topic. In 1958, a book was published in Russia. It listed ways to overthrow America. One of those ways was to get the Americans away from their God and morals. They knew if Americans kept their morals and beliefs in God, the United States would remain the most richest, powerful, and religious country in the world. They knew America would fall apart from within and lose their strong position if they could rip God out of their values and schools. As you see, they accomplished this goal.

Five years later, the Supreme Court ruled that prayers would not be in any public school. The following year, it ruled to take the Bible out of schools. This is one of the beginning acts by the United States of America, which showed hatred towards God. In this country, we have over eighty percent of the population who say they are Christians or believe in God. The question is; how did the minority of the people get control of the foundation from which this country began? What happened to introducing a bill for the Americans to vote with a democratic system? How did one person have so much influence to convince the Supreme Court? The ruling was eight to one in the favor of taking prayer out of schools across an entire nation. The person winning victory in the Supreme Court suffered a brutal death with some of their family members.

In the Bible, when countries took God out of their governments, those nations crumbled. I am watching our country fall apart. Our children are killing each other at school. They are disrespectful and very rude. A lot of them are without morals. Our forefathers stressed in the Constitution how important it was for our nation to have morals, values, and God. How could we let one cry turn us into a condemned land? The Word says:

"The wicked shall be turned into hell, and all the nations that forget God."
Psalms 9:17 KJV

Taking God out of schools was the most dangerous thing that our nation did. The first consecutive eighteen years our average ACT and SAT test scores dropped after this ruling. The United States is no longer the top country in the world for educating our young children. We are no longer the top country in the world to fear. Now, it takes us ten plus years to try to win wars. Our nation needs to open their eyes before it gets worse. God has already destroyed cities and nations. The Bibles states:

"And that the whole land thereof is brimstone, and salt, and burning, that it is not sown, nor beareth, nor any grass growth therein, like the overthrow of Sodom, and Gomorah, Admah, and Zeboim, which the Lord overthrew in his anger, and in his wrath:
Even all nations shall say, Wherefore, hath the Lord done thus unto this land? What meaneth the heat of this great anger?
Then men shall say, Because they have forsaken the covenant of the Lord God of their fathers, which he made with them when he brought them forth out of the land of Egypt:
For they went and served other gods, and worshiped them, gods whom they knew not, and whom he had not given unto them:
And the anger of the Lord was kindled against this land, to bring upon it all curses that are written in this book."
Deuteronomy 29:23-27 KJV

The Bible was one of the books used to teach our children how to read at the same time it taught them morals. The early settlers made sure the Word was a part of their curriculum. The Bible was also a tool for learning at the first colleges in our country. Prayer and worship were also included as a part of the student's day.

Nowadays, our nation lives in fear of sending our children to school. We never know if the school in our neighborhood will be in a time of mourning and grieving by the end of our day. I have been stunned at some of the brutal killings at schools with machine guns. When I was a child, we never had to worry about intruders coming and wasting a defenseless class. This has spread to other public places such as movie theaters, fast food restaurants, churches, home, and our jobs. Where is there a safe place? There is not a safe place in our nation or in the world. Satan has convinced this nation, there is no need for God to be in the government. He has convinced a nation to hate God.

I can see this so clearly and some of you can see it. If you were born before the Supreme Court banned prayers out of schools, it is quite noticeable. When you are in tune with God's spirit, you can see we are living in the last days. The commandments, which God called immoral, are becoming laws. There seems to be nothing that the majority can do about it. The minority of people are finding glitches in the Constitution, which said to keep the church separated from the state. Since this was over two hundred years ago, they say times have changed.

One of the laws they changed, say that a man can marry a man and a woman can marry a woman. God clearly gave the guidelines for marriage and union in the Bible. It says:

"Thou shall not lie with mankind, as with womankind: it is abomination."
Leviticus 18:22 KJV

Furthermore, it says:

"If a man also lie with mankind, as he lieth with a woman, both of them have committed an abomination: they shall surely be put to death; their blood shall be upon them."
Leviticus 20:13" KJV

If you need a New Testament verse, it states:

"For this cause God gave them up unto vile affections: for even their women did change the natural use into that which is against nature:
And likewise also the men, leaving the natural use of the woman, burned in their lust one toward another: men with mem working that which is unseemly, and receiving in themselves that recompense of their error which was meet."
Romans 1:26-27 LJV

The laws of the land are changing giving the people permission to sin against God. The laws are making the wrong right and the right wrong. The majority of the people do not control the laws. The laws are changing in front of our faces. We all sin, but our laws should not conform to our sins. God's principles still stand.

"Woe to them that call evil good, and good evil: that put darkness for light, and light for darkness; that put bitter for sweet, and sweet for bitter!"
Isaiah 5:20 KJV

The people making these new regulations fail to

realize that God does not change. He is the same yesterday, today, and forever. God is the truth and nothing but the truth. Human beings are the ones who lie. Lying is not one of God's characteristics.

"God is not a man, that he should lie; neither the son of man, that he should repent: hath he said, and shall he not do it?"
Numbers 23:19 KJV

When God stated what would happen to a nation that turned against Him in the Bible, it occurred as He said. While viewing the news, we often see our court-systems let the guilty go free. I observed our nation take away parental rights to discipline their children. The parents can now go to jail for their children's behavior. I witnessed children disrespecting their parents simply because they knew they could get away with it. Families are killing and disowning each other.

Yes, we are living in the last days and Jesus is soon to return. I know God is giving us every opportunity to change and has me writing a book of this magnitude. It is easy to see all of these things unfold. In 2013, I observed our nation divide itself by shutting down the government. This hurt our economy. In 2015, the senate sent a letter to Iran against the President of the United States concerning the nuclear negotiations. The Word clearly states:

"And if a kingdom be divided against itself, that kingdom cannot stand.
And if a house be divided against itself, that house cannot stand.

And if Satan rise up against himself, and be divided, he cannot stand, but hath an end."
Mark 3:24-26 KJV

I believe our nation needs to get back to the foundation from which this country was established. The nation needs God. When we become our own gods, we hate God. We need to be more particular about the movies and television shows we watch. The movies, which used to be innocent, are no longer blameless. We need to guard what we watch, read, hear, and see so that there are no opportunities for the enemy to trick or deceive us into breaking God's commandments.

I have seen drastic changes since I was a child. The superheroes costumes used to be bright and colorful. They never killed anybody; they just fought the villains and put them in jail. Nowadays, the superheroes' costumes, character, city, and background are dark and anomalous. You cannot distinguish whom the superhero and the villains are because there is so much darkness and killing. Is this what our children should be watching? Not to mention, we use God's name in vain. I have observed children's cartoons and movies cleaning up God's name in vain by using the initials instead. Really? We are sending the wrong message to our children. We need to get rid of these excuses; "It is okay as long as I am not doing it." "It does not bother me." In addition, "It is just a movie." These statements are tricks of the enemy. He is manipulating our behavior from the thoughts he has planted in our minds and we are accepting these concepts. The Bibles says in the Ten Commandments:

I Hate God

"Thou shalt not take the name of the Lord thy God in vain: for the Lord will not hold him guiltless that taketh his name in vain."
Deuteronomy 5:11 KJV

I stay away from all movies, which uses God's name in vain, because God gave me this scenario. If someone were talking bad about your parents, would you let them? Would you stop them? Would you act as if nothing happened? Would you walk away with anger? Would you have no feelings about it at all? It is offensive to speak against our Heavenly Father and use His name in vain. My spirit personally becomes disturbed. Even if I wanted to know what happened at the end of a good movie, once I hear God's name in vain, I get up and leave the theater. If I am in control of the movie at home, I turn it off.

Some of the authors, who wrote the Bible, did not use God's name. Traditionally, Jews felt they were unworthy to speak God's name and they never used God's name in vain. They reverenced God and decided it was better to omit God's name to honor Him.

Toys, tablets, cell phones, iPads, and video games are gods in the house of the Lord. Parents and guardians are allowing the children to play these games at church. They are allowing them to ignore our Heavenly Father in His own house. Yes, the children are just children, but we need to teach them to give their time to God. There are plenty of opportunities for children to play their games outside of church. They can't play with these items in school, pre-school, and nursery school can they? No, they have to wait until recess to play because some time is set aside for them to sit in their seats and learn. We must treat God's house the same way. God is not pleased with this behavior of letting children entertain themselves with their gods. Unless they are reading the Bible from their cells phones and iPads with the minister, they need to wait until after church to play with their video games and toys. He said that He is a jealous God. The Word says:

"Thou shalt have no other gods before me.
Thou shalt not make unto thee any graven image, or any likeness of any thing that is in heaven above, or that is in the earth beneath, or that is in the water under the earth:
Thou shalt not bow down thyself to them, nor serve them: for I the Lord thy God is a jealous God, visiting the iniquity of the fathers upon the children unto the third and fourth generation of them that hate me;
And showing mercy unto thousands of them that love me, and keep my commandments."
Exodus 20:3-6 KJV

Moreover, the Bible states:

"Train up a child in the way he should go: and when he is old, he will not depart from it."
Proverbs 22:6 KJV

We have to teach the children that God is first. Letting them play with toys and video games at church is teaching them that it is okay to ignore and hate God. These items become the children's gods since they do not have to pay attention while the Word of God comes forth through the message. The children are our future.

What will the future become if these children text and play video games during church with their children? For some people, going to church is just going through the motions. Make the children pay attention to the sermon. Ask them questions and have conversations to let them tell you what they learned. This will save their souls. The games will do nothing for their salvation. We are responsible for our children's upbringing.

We do not need to help society lead our children astray. We need to teach them to respect the House of God. Parents need to have family time to read the Bible together. The Bible is our guide to our deliverance. It is time to evaluate our lives to make sure we are not guilty of making other items our gods in our lives.

I see a world that has driven themselves far from God. I was one of them at one time. When I backslid from God, I showed the Lord hatred without even knowing it. This revelation was there; however, I could not see it in the state I was living.

So many of us are still blind. We do not want to see, we do not know to see, or we are being openly rebellious. I do not know how much longer God is going to warn us, but I do know He is doing everything in His power to give us every opportunity to repent. He is giving us another chance to give up a life of hating Him.

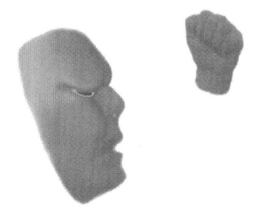

DO YOU HATE GOD

Most people will not say they hate God, if you ask them. Some people are not aware they hate the Lord. If you are living in sin, disobeying God, practicing witchcraft, and not praying, you hate God. This is why God wanted me to write 'I Hate God.' He wants you to evaluate your life. You will know without a doubt if you hate God. No one will have to tell you because your spirit will convict you. If you do, you can correct your life.

There were two examples of hating God written in this book. One example was my father admitting to himself, others, and God, the hatred he had for Him from his heart. I was the second example; I lived my life in sin and denied that I hated God. I was living a lie thinking I loved God. It is better to be the first example because the fact was evident. My father was a better man for telling the truth. I on the other hand, did not know I hated God. It took someone to tell me directly, "You hate God," for me to start accepting the truth.

Even then, it was hard for me to digest. The Word of God was letting me know; I, in fact, hated God. I was filthy with sin. According to the Word of God, there is no way to love Him in that condition. I was serving and loving the wrong master. I cannot stress this Bible verse enough:

"No man can serve two masters: for either he will hate the one, and love the other; or else he will hold to the one, and despise the other. Ye cannot serve God and mammon."
Matthew 6:24 KJV

There is no arguing with God on this subject. The Word of God speaks to those of us who will listen. As you have seen with my father's and my stories, God will prove Himself to you if you ask. I would recommend that you be more respectful when you pursue to get your answer from the Lord. He will prove to you that He does exist. Try Him and see for yourself. Do not stay in the state of hating God because you do not believe. Ask God to help you to believe. This story tells you from the Word how to ask for such help and other important points, which may help you.

"And one of the multitude answered and said, Master, I have brought unto thee my son, which hath a dumb spirit;
And wheresoever he taketh him, he teareth him: and he foameth, and gnasheth with his teeth, and pineth away: and I spake to thy disciples that they should cast him

out; and they could not.

He answereth him, and said, O faithless generation, how long shall I be with you? how long shall I suffer you? bring him unto me.

And they brought him unto him: and when he saw him, straightway the spirit tare him; and he fell on the ground, wallowed foaming.

And he asked his father, How long is it ago since this came unto him? And he said, of a child.

And ofttimes it hath cast him into the fire, and into the waters, to destroy him: but if thou canst do any thing, have compassion on us, and help us.

Jesus said unto him, If thou canst believe, all things are possible to him that believeth.

And straightway the father of the child cried out, and said with tears, Lord, I believe; help thou mine unbelief.

When Jesus saw that the people came running together, he rebuked the foul spirit, saying unto him, Thou dumb and deaf spirit, I charge thee, come out of him, and enter no more into him.

And the spirit cried, and rent him sore, and came out of him: and he was as one dead; insomuch that many said, He is dead.

But Jesus took him by the hand, and lifted him up; and he arose.

And when he was come into the house, his disciples asked him privately, Why could not we cast him out?

And he said unto them, This kind can come forth by nothing, but by prayer and fasting."

Mark 9:17-29 KJV

If you do not believe, ask God to help your unbelief believe. It is that simple. Whenever I felt like I did not have enough faith about something, I asked God to make my unbelief believe. He did just that and He will do it for you. Just as Jesus helped the man with the son unbelief to believe, He will help you to believe.

God will not overpower you. Your freewill prevents Him from doing that. You must go to God. Those of you who do not believe there is a God, you can also ask God for proof of His presence. He will verify His existence. He has proven Himself many times to man and yet many men do not believe.

I have seen angels so I would be out of my mind if I do not believe. Oh, and let us not forget my inner body experience. This is my utmost evidence because God controlled my body for a couple of hours of my life and I could not do anything about it.

Speaking of my inner body event, if God wanted to control us to worship Him, He could. We would be walking around this earth as the Lord controlled our every movement. The choice would not be ours. We would have to believe He existed. We would not have any say so about what we would eat, drink, watch, do, pray, or say. He could have made us His robots; however, He gave us full self-control. Instead, He wanted us to choose to love and worship Him. We would have to deal with it if God decided to control us.

I do not take for granted anymore that we have freewill. I am happy and honored to serve God. You can be happy serving God too, but you have to make the decision for yourself. Do you love God enough to obey His will? If not, you hate God. I know this is a blunt statement but I have to obey what God wants me to write. The Word of God has been sugar coated long enough in today's society. You hardly ever hear the

Heaven and Hell sermons.

I used to hear those kinds of sermons as a child all of the time. They scared me straight. The preachers did not hold back any punches. They preached it whether you liked it or not. Most of all, the church was still packed. Small and large churches were crowded. This tells me that the people really wanted to hear the Word of God to keep them on the straight and narrow road to Heaven. The Word says:

"And he said unto them, He that hath ears to hear, let him hear."
Mark 4:9 KJV

It is up to you to hear this or not hear this. It is up to you to believe by exercising your faith. God left this up to your judgement. However, if you go to Hell, remember you wanted to go there because of your decision while you are living. You volunteered. You will not be able to blame anyone else. Please select wisely since the outcome is eternal. Your actions will determine if you hate God. As you read my story in this book, just because I did not say I hated God, did not mean that I did not hate Him. My lifestyle told the real story. I did in fact hate God while I was drowning in my iniquities. Your life is a reflection of how you feel about God.

Get into a strong Bible based church. Learn the Word of God. Go to Bible study and allow yourself to learn with a teachable spirit. Do not depend on someone else's interpretation alone because they may be making a mistake. Look up the verses and create a relationship with your Heavenly Father. Ask questions when you need understanding. Study and seek God's face for yourself.

Over time, my father began to let hatred melt from his heart. He began to see that God did not do these evil things to him. If we just sit down and analyze the situation, we will find that God does not commit wicked acts. Humankind's choices will allow man to be as corrupt as he wants to be. The enemy thrives on us to destroy ourselves when he enters our minds and hearts. It is up to us to resist the temptations.

I am glad God gave me so many opportunities. If He had not, I would be doomed to live eternity in the fiery pits of Hell. The Lord looked beyond my faults. He forgave me for hating Him. He forgave my father for hating Him. He wants to forgive you for hating Him. If you hate God right now, He is waiting and knocking at the door of your heart. The Bible says:

"Behold, I stand at the door, and knock: if any man hear my voice, and open the door, I will come in to him, and will sup with him, and he with me."
Revelation 3:20 KJV

Will you open the door? Will you let Him into your heart? You and your freewill are the only things standing in your way. Choose to serve God. The signs of the end of time are everywhere. These days, it is not safe to go to church or anywhere else. They have no respect for the Lord's house. Let us face it, nowhere on this planet is safe. Give your life over to God. Find God for yourself. Keep searching until you find Him. It says in the Word:

"Ask, and it shall be given you; seek, and ye shall find; knock, and it shall be opened unto you:
For every one that asketh receiveth; and he that seeketh findeth; and to him that knocketh it shall be opened.
Or what man is there of you, whom if his son ask bread, will he give him a stone?
Or if he ask a fish, will he give him a serpent?
If ye then, being evil, know how to give good gifts unto your children, how much more shall your Father which is in heaven give good things to them that ask Him?"
Matthew 7:7-11 KJV

All you have to do is ask Him and you will receive Him. Seek Him and you will find Him. Knock at His door and He will open it. Beware of pastors who lead their sheep astray. The Bible says:

"Woe be unto the pastors that destroy and scatter the sheep of my pasture! saith the Lord."
Jeremiah 23:1 KJV

Additionally, it says if you are a good shepherd, you will:

"Feed the flock of God which is among you, taking the oversight thereof, not by constraint, but willingly; not for filthy lucre, but of a ready mind;
Neither as being lords over God's heritage, but being examples to the flock.
And when the chief Shepherd shall appear, ye shall receive a crown of glory that fadeth not away."
1 Peter 5:2-4 KJV

I Hate God

The shepherd is supposed to feed the flock not lead them astray. Everyone will be accountable for his or her own actions. Please do not be a part of the wrong category before God, whether you are the sheep or the shepherd. It is dangerous.

Many of you say you love God, but at the same time, you do not love your family members, neighbors, or your enemies. Many of us have siblings and other family members, who are still angry about something in the past. It is time to forgive and move on to what is happening today. Some of us do not even know what we did. Some of us are upset with our siblings because of childhood memories. Let it go and forgive. The sibling was a child too and we know a child's maturity level should not be accountable as if he or she was an adult. Even if they were an adult, we still have to forgive if we want God to forgive us. Some of us are upset because our family member did not agree with us about something. Everyone is different and has his or her own mental thought process. Respect their thoughts and let it go. Agree to disagree while still loving your family. Do not let this animosity stay in your hearts because if you do, you cannot love God whom you have not seen. If you do, you hate God. The Word says:

"If a man say, I love God, and hateth his brother, he is a liar: for he that loveth not his brother whom he hath seen, how can he love God whom he hath not seen?
And this commandment have we from him, that he who loveth God love his brother also."
1 John 4:20-21 KJV

We must love our neighbor as we love ourselves.

This includes people we do not know. God does not ask us to do this; He commands us to do this. A commandment does not give you a choice. It is the second commandment. In this commandment, God also told us to love ourselves. You do not love yourself when you constantly beat yourself up over guilt or shame about something you did or did not do. Remain confident in yourself that you have overcome your iniquities and faults. Learn from your mistakes. It says:

"And Jesus answered him, the first of all the commandments is, Hear, O Israel; The Lord our God is one Lord:
And thou shalt love the Lord thy God with all thy heart, and with all thy soul, and with all thy mind, and with all thy strength: this is the first commandment.
And the second is like, namely this; Thou shalt love thy neighbor as thyself. There is none other commandment greater than these."
Mark 12:29-31 KJV

Loving our enemies is one of the hardest things that God told us to do. How can you love someone who has done an evil act towards you? They may have stolen from you, killed a loved one, raped you, broke your heart, and the list goes on, but we still have to forgive and love them. Without forgiving and loving them, we hate God. Do not let the pain make your heart fill up with hatred. Jesus displayed the most love for His enemies in this passage.

"And one of them smote the servant of the high priest, and cut off his right ear.

And Jesus answered and said, Suffer ye thus far. And he touched his ear, and healed him."
Luke 22:50-51 KJV

Look at the love Jesus had for His enemy. He still healed the soldier knowing what His fate was in his hands. It doesn't even matter if this is a difficult task for you; obey God so that you can heal from your emotional pain. Hating the person is not going to change the fact that the incident happened; so let it go. God will deal with them; this is not your job or battle. You are only responsible for forgiving and loving your enemy. If your rival needs anything and you have it, you are required to give it to them. The Bible says:

"Ye have heard that it hath been said, Thou shalt love your neighbor, and hate thine enemy.
But I say unto you, Love your enemies, bless them that curse you, do good to them that hate you, and pray for them which despitefully use you, and persecute you:"
Matthew 5:43-44

Furthermore, it states:

"Dearly beloved, avenge not yourselves, but rather give place unto wrath: for it is written, Vengeance is mine; I will repay, saith the Lord.
Therefore if thine enemy hunger, feed him; if he thirst, give him drink: for in so doing thou shalt heap coals of fire on his head.
Be not overcome of evil, but overcome evil with good."
Romans 12:19-21 KJV

Those of you, who are backsliding, please come back to the Lord. If you are anything like I was, you know you are missing the Lord in your life. You hate God as long as you are backsliding. God still loves you and He will forgive you. Come back, His arms are open wide for you. You know inside of your heart, it is time to give up your worldly ways. This Bible verse may help you.

"Turn, O backsliding children, saith the Lord; for I am married unto you: and I will take you one of a city, and two of a family, and I will bring you to Zion."
Jeremiah 3:14 KJV

Wow, backsliders are married to God. This means, no matter what you have done in your backslidden state, God is waiting for you to come back to Him. This is so powerful. Do not keep living in fear of your death. Repent and show God you love Him. Don't express any more hatred towards God.

We need to realize that our bodies are the temples of God. We are committing adultery with the temple of God. We are stealing with the temple of God. We are telling lies with the temple of God. We are worshipping false gods with the temple of God. We are hurting people and our spouses with the temple of God. We are killing with the temple of God. We are raping others with the temple of God. We are dishonoring our parents and elders with the temple of God. We are leading others astray with the temple of God. We are using witchcraft with the temple of God. We are putting unclean things in our bodies with the temple of God. We are cussing with the temple of God. We are watching pornography with the temple of God. We are

131

committing suicide with the temple of God. We are using God's name in vain with the temple of God. We hate others and God with the temple of God. We are unforgiving with the temple of God. We refuse to believe God exists with the temple of God. We are being hypocrites with the temple of God. We are backsliding with the temple of God. We are sinning on purpose and unknowingly with the temple of God. It is not too late to change and repent. Please do not keep doing these acts with the temple of God. Respect the Lord's house and His temple. Your body is the temple of God. The Word says:

"What? Know ye not that your body is the temple of the Holy Ghost which is in you, which ye have of God, and ye are not your own?
For ye are bought with a price: therefore glorify God in your body, and in your spirit, which are God's."
1 Corinthians 6:19-20 KJV

Glorify the Lord instead of sinning against the Lord with your body. Do not hate God anymore with your lifestyle. Surrender everything to Him. Living for God is rewarding. God sees your heart. He sees everything. I did not know my body was God's temple for the majority of my sinful days. This scripture made a difference because I did not want to treat God's temple in a corrupt manner and disrespect it. I hope this is the same for you. Imagine someone coming into your temple or house, and messing it all up with a lot of filth. This is how the reflection of our lives, are treating God's temple. It is time to clean house and respect God's temple, which is your body.

When you are giving God the glory for what He has done for you, testify with utmost respect. For instance, cussing while you are testifying sends the wrong signals. Are you thankful for what God has done for you or are you just talking? Do this math problem. Add positive one and negative one. What answer did you calculate? The answer is zero. The ones cancel each other out, leaving nothing. Do not cancel your testimonies out with worldly conversation. God is too pure to edify Him with cuss words surrounding His great acts and miracles. Give Him the glory and honor He deserves. Keep in mind, God doesn't have to do anything for us; however, He does because He loves us.

We all need to be careful; do not speak about God with a false tongue. Telling lies about God or telling a lie in the name of the Lord could be damnation for our souls. Throughout my lifetime, I have heard these statements. 'God sent me my mate even though I am still married. He understands and no one can tell me that God did not send him or her into my life.' God is not going to contradict His own Word. It says:

"Thou shalt not commit adultery."
Exodus 20:14 KJV

God is holy and cannot sin. This means He cannot lie. The Word says:

"God is not a man, that he should lie; neither the son of man, that he should repent: hath he said, and shall he not do it? Or hath he spoken, and shall he not make it good?"
Number 23:19 KJV

Additionally, it says:

"Then the Lord said unto me, "The prophets prophesy lies in my name: I sent them not, neither have I commanded them, neither spake unto them: they prophesy unto you a false vision and divination, and a thing of nought, and the deceit of their heart.
Therefore thus saith the Lord concerning the prophets that prophesy in my name, and I sent them not, yet they say, Sword and famine shall not be in this land; By sword and famine shall those prophets be consumed."
Jeremiah 14:14-15 KJV

Also the Word says:

"Being filled with all unrighteousness, fornication, wickedness, covetousness, maliciousness; full of envy, murder, debate, deceit, malignity; whisperers,
Backbiters, haters of God, despiteful, proud, boasters, inventors of evil things, disobedient to parents,
Without understanding, covenant-breakers, without natural affection, implacable, unmerciful:
Who knowing the judgement of God, that they which commit such things are worthy of death, not only do the same, but have pleasure in them that do them.
Romans 1:29-32

God is not going to go against the laws in His Word. If He did, God would be a liar. He is perfect. The Word plainly states that we cannot commit adultery. If we do, we are rebelling against God's laws and we hate Him. When we take it to another level and lie on God by saying, "God gave me my mate," in the midst of our adulterous or fornication sins, God will bring us to our destruction. This also goes for anyone prophesizing to anyone falsely in the name of the Lord. We have to be careful of what we say about God. Please do not do things in the name of the Lord or behind the cloth. The Bible says:

"Lying lips are abomination to the Lord: but they that deal truly are his delight."
Proverbs 12:22 KJV

Be cautious when you are speaking when it concerns God. The truth is pleasing to Him.

Realizing that you hate God if you are a sinner, backslider, or hypocrite, is a hard pill to swallow. Trust me; it was not easy for me either to accept this fact. Once I came to this awareness, I repented. You too will need to repent and begin your new life. Evaluate your life thoroughly to make sure that you do not hate God.

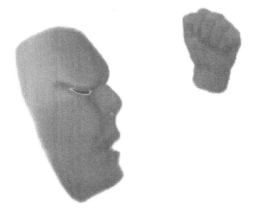

STILL TIME TO REPENT

When I was backsliding, I knew what my fate would be if I had died; but I kept sinning anyway because I was comfortable with my life. I was having too much fun. Nothing is worse than when the Superior Being reminds you constantly to obey Him. I felt guilty after all of my sins. How is it that I did not feel guilty before or during my iniquities? The answer to this question is; the forbidden fruit looked good to me so I wanted and tasted the fruit.

Someone told me one day, "I know God doesn't want me to do this, but I am going to do it anyway."

This was nothing but a rebellious spirit. Their heart was cold and they were not willing to obey the Lord. In other words, they were set on sinning against God. The Lord is not going to force you to serve or obey Him.

This same person also said, "God gave us freewill."

Yes, He did. Do you know what? We do not have

freewill when the consequences happen and follow our decisions. If we go to Hell when we die, we selected to go there if we refuse to serve God while we lived. Think about it; we choose whether we sin or not. We decide whether to believe the words in the Bible. We show whether we believe God is real or not. We make the choice to obey God. We select which way our destiny will go. It will be our fault if we go to Hell and it will be our reward if we go to Heaven. Freewill carries a price. It carries a great compensation if we make the right judgement and a bad consequence if we make the wrong decision.

I thank God for allowing me all of the chances He has given me. The last time that I backslid, God told me I had no more chances. He told me if I went back to my old ways again, I would die in sin. I have not relapsed since and I have been getting closer to God every day. If God has given you a warning, I would suggest you take heed. The Lord is not joking because He is very serious. God has given us warning after warning, but it is up to us to see the signs. If different people come to you with the same message, maybe you should consider God is trying to tell you something.

Some people go to church on Sunday while continuing their same sinful behavior. Going to church alone is not enough. It is only one part of the development. We must make an effort to live as the scriptures instructed. The Holy Spirit is our teacher and comforter. He fills us with God's love and word. We grieve the Holy Spirit when we sin. God did not give us a license to sin all we want by letting His Son suffer through the crucifixion process.

Some people have told me, "Once you except Jesus

as your Savior, you are saved no matter what else you do." This is a mockery for everything Jesus suffered on Calvary. The Word says:

"Be not deceived; God is not mocked: for whatsoever a man soweth, that shall he also reap."
Galatians 6:7 KJV

Yes, God will forgive you, but we can't take grace for granted. The price that Christ paid was excessive and beyond what we deserved. His crucifixion, death, and resurrection were gifts of God's mercy for us. Because of this, we should not continue living in our iniquities after we have accepted Christ as our Savior. The Bible says:

"What shall we say then? Shall we continue in sin, that grace may abound?
God forbid. How shall we that are dead to sin, live any longer therein?
Romans 6:1-2 KJV

We cannot continue in our sin sick state. Jesus' blood paid for our salvation. At some point, we will need to change our sinful behavior. Our guilt overpowers us when we realize that we need to repent. Do not ignore these feelings of conviction. Knowing that we are wrong is our first step in the process of repenting. The Word says:

"That if thou confess with thy mouth the Lord Jesus, and shalt believe in thine heart that God hath raised him from the dead, thou shalt be saved.

For with the heart man believeth unto righteousness; and with the mouth confession is made unto salvation."
Romans 10:9-10 KJV

Confess your iniquities. On page 147 of this book, there is a confession prayer. Once you have confessed your sins before the Lord, you will need to resist temptations. The Word says:

"Submit yourselves therefore to God. Resist the devil, and he will flee from you."
James 4:7 KJV

We cannot resist our enticing sins on our own. If we fail, we must repent until we get it right. We must gather up the strength to counterattack the enemy with the Word of God. We have to pray without ceasing until we overcome our flesh. We may have to fast to increase our strength and faith. The Bible says:

"And he said unto them, this kind can come forth by nothing, but by prayer and fasting."
Mark 9:29 KJV

Remember, God knows your heart. When you repent, it must be sincere. Remorse is the next step in the process of repenting and you must humble yourself before the Lord. If you can, pray on your knees. This is the most humbling position. The Word says:

"For it is written, As I live, saith the Lord, every knee shall bow to me, and every tongue shall confess to God."

Romans 14:11 KJV

Additionally it says:

"If my people, which are called by my name, shall humble themselves, and pray, and seek my face, and turn from their wicked ways; then will I hear from heaven, and will forgive their sin, and will heal their land."
2 Chronicles 7:14 KJV

You have to be willing to submit yourself to the Lord. No one can force you. The decision is an intimate experience between you and God. I encourage you to increase your prayer life and spend time with God. As long as you are living, there is time to repent. Follow your heart.

You must repent to God. You may go to a church official to assist you with the process of repenting to God; however, you will also have to pray for your atonement yourself. Confess your sins to God and know He has forgiven you. The Word says:

"I acknowledged my sin unto thee, and mine iniquity have I not hid. I said, I will confess my transgressions unto the Lord; and thou forgavest the iniquity of my sin."
Psalm 32:5 KJV

God's forgiveness is a relief. You will find peace once you have God's forgiveness because He has justified you. Look at this verse:

I Hate God

"Therefore being justified by faith, we have peace with God through our Lord Jesus Christ:"
Romans 5:1 KJV

It is time for you to forgive your iniquities. This is a crucial step. Many times, we don't forgive ourselves. We live a life of torment for years when God has already thrown our sins in the sea of forgiveness. The Bible says:

"He will turn again, he will have compassion upon us; he will subdue our iniquities; and thou wilt cast all their sins into the depths of the sea."
Micah 7:19 KJV

When you throw something into the depths of the sea, this means it is inaccessible and you cannot see it. It is gone. See how wonderful the Lord is. He has put your sins in a place where He is not thinking about them. The time has come for you to move on and learn from your mistakes. The Bible says:

"For the scripture saith, "Whosoever believeth on him shall not be ashamed."
Roman 10:11 KJV

The last step is to trust God. If the Lord says He has forgiven you, believe Him. He gives you strength in the time of trouble and temptations. God will deliver you if you ask Him.

"The Lord knoweth how to deliver the godly out of temptations, and to reserve the unjust unto the day of

judgment to be punished:"
2 Peter 2:9 KJV

Furthermore, it reads:

"For whosoever shall call upon the name of the Lord shall be saved."
Romans 10:13 KJV

Make time for God. Serve Him with everything you have. Don't be too busy to pray. Allow time in your schedule to praise the Lord even in the midst of chaos. Read the Bible every day. No matter what is going on, set aside some time for the Lord. If we do not do this, we hate God. Satan loves when we are too busy to worship God. He gains power over us as we make it easier for him to devour us.

"Be sober, be vigilant; because your adversary the devil, as a roaring lion, walketh about, seeking whom he may devour:"
1 Peter 5:8 KJV

We need to put on the full armor of God. This is very important. The Word says:

"Finally, my brethren, be strong in the Lord, and in the power of his might.
Put on the whole armor of God, that ye may be able to stand against the wiles of the devil.
For we wrestle not against flesh and blood, but against principalities, against powers, against the rulers of the darkness of this world, against spiritual wickedness in

high places.
Wherefore take unto you the whole armor of God that ye may be able to withstand in the evil day, and having done all, to stand.
Stand therefore, having your loins girt about with truth, and having on the breastplate of righteousness;
And your feet shod with the preparation of the gospel of peace;
Above all, taking the shield of faith, wherewith ye shall be able to quench all the fiery darts of the wicked.
And take the helmet of salvation, and the sword of the Spirit, which is the word of God:
Praying always with all prayer and supplication in the Spirit, and watching thereunto with all perseverance and supplication for all saints;"
Ephesians 6:10-18 KJV

With repentance, you will have God's protection and strength. If you stay corrupted, you are very vulnerable. There is so much more that the enemy can do to you if you refuse to surrender your all to Christ. Additionally, the Heavenly Father has rewards to make this journey worth our efforts. The Bible says:

"Rejoice, and be exceeding glad: for great is your reward in heaven: for so persecuted they the prophets which were before you."
Matthew 5:12 KJV

Additionally it says:

"Blessed is the man that endureth temptation: for when he is tried, he shall receive the crown of life, which the

Lord hath promised to them that love him."
James 1:12 KJV

When I was running from God and living a life of sin, I did not pray. What was the point of praying if I was going to do the same thing over the next day? Some prayers are in vain and I knew this. The Bible says:

"Now we know that God heareth not sinners: but if any man be a worshipper of God, and doeth his will, him he heareth."
John 9:31 KJV

I was not going to live right any time soon, so I just did not pray. I felt it was stupid to pray if God wasn't going to hear me. As I looked back at this period during my life, I was unwise and naïve. I did not realize how dangerous this was for my soul. I acknowledge now that I had a rebellious and stubborn spirit. I hope this testimony helps someone who is in the same predicament that I was in during this time in my life.

I heard a great sermon one day, which made a difference in my life. It was about the soul. The minister said that when we sin, our soul is crying out because it knows our destiny. The soul is begging for our flesh to do the right thing; however, it has no control. Our conscious mind and the flesh have the control. The only way to overpower them is to repent and serve God. It will still be hard; but you are giving your soul a chance to live eternally in Heaven.

As you begin to build your strength against any weaknesses in your life, eventually your temptations will begin to fade away with God leading you. The Holy

Ghost will become dominant inside of your spirit. You will conquer your iniquities. The uneasiness in your heart will help you to resist your greatest temptations. Your inner spirit will begin to transform and it will stop hating God.

Once I heard this sermon, my thoughts concentrated on my soul. I did not want to make my soul suffer from any of my fleshly actions. I was responsible for its destination. This was and is a big responsibility, which I was not aware I had.

After I did a self-evaluation, it was time for me to repent. It was time for me to forgive others and myself. I had to change my ways. I began to love others. Most of all, I fell in love with the Lord and began to serve Him. Repenting was the first thing I had to do. I can say that I have more joy and peace during the midst of my storms and temptations. It is worth every breath I breathe to serve the Lord.

In conclusion, I pray if you have not been atoned for your sins, that you will soon become remorseful before it is too late. Ask God to forgive you for the sake of your soul. Repent and serve the Lord with everything you have. Serve God and take the opportunity that the Lord has given you. If you keep rebelling and living in a life of sin, you in fact, hate God.

Save your soul. Your sin sick soul is dying because of the sins you're not fighting. Evaluate your life. Do you hate God? If you do, do not live another day hating God, whether you are verbally saying it or physically living a life of sin. Worship Him with all of your soul. Most of all, love God with all of your heart in every action with your life that He has given you. To God be the Glory for your unconditional love for God.

Prayer of Repentance and Confession

Heavenly Father,

I humble myself before You. Please forgive me for of all of my sins. I am asking You to have mercy on me because I have sinned against You. I confess my transgressions. I believe that Your Son Jesus died on the cross for my iniquities. Forgive me for taking His blood for granted and for hating You verbally or with my actions. Please cleanse me Father. Thank You for giving me the opportunity to serve and worship You Lord. I thank You because I know that I do not deserve this chance, but because of Your loving kindness, mercy, and grace, You have given me this time to turn my life around for Your glory. Thank You for reaching out to me and showing me the way. Please guide me and give me the strength to resist temptation. I cry out to You Father because I know I can do better. I need You in my life and I am ready to do Your will. I surrender my life to You. I accept Jesus as my personal Savior. Thank You God for Your forgiveness. You are worthy of all praises and I love You Lord. In Jesus' name amen.

If you have said this prayer with sincerity before God, you have been born again and you are now one of His children. Congratulations!

"But after that faith is come, we are no longer under a schoolmaster.
For ye are all the children of God by in Christ Jesus."
Galatians 3:25-26 KJV

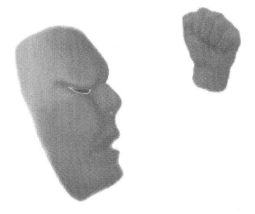

EIGHTY-TWO CUPCAKES

In April of 2015, I was fasting before Easter. I had one more week to fast. I was planning my meal that I would make the following Monday. I wanted to make something special for my son. This meant that I was going to make one of Bob J's favorite cakes. I decided to make him a carrot cake. I also planned to cook some rolls made from scratch, barbeque ribs, macaroni and cheese, sweet potato casserole, and green beans. While I was in this deep thought of planning the meal, my father called.

My father was excited and asked, "What are you doing Daughter?

I replied, "I am planning the meal that I am going to cook after my fast Dad."

He was curious and enquired, "What are you going to cook?"

I proceeded to tell him the menu and he stopped me

as soon as I said carrot cake.

My father was in a state of shock and said, "What? Did you say you are making carrot cake?

Laughing I responded, "Yes Sir."

"Are you making it from scratch?"

"Yes Dad, I always make my cakes from scratch."

My father was fascinated at the same time he was saddened. He knew that since I lived in Georgia and he lived in Iowa, there was no chance on this earth that he could get any carrot cake.

He reluctantly stated, "Boy, I wish I was there. Carrot cake is my most favorite cake in the world."

Stunned at his statement, I asked, "Dad, did you say carrot cake is your favorite cake?"

"Yes, and I haven't had it in years. Is carrot cake your favorite too?"

My father's passion for carrot cake moved me and I knew that I could fix his situation. I knew how it felt to miss something that you really love. Now, it was time to give my father a chance to eat a quality dessert. I never have any boxed cake mixes or canned icing in my pantry. I love the old-fashioned taste of cooking from scratch. I don't care if it is pie, cookies, or cake; there is nothing like the flavor from the good old days. My father was missing the carrot cake from his past. I was ecstatic that I could show my father how special he is to me simply by giving him the pleasure of waking up his taste buds.

Mysteriously I answered, "No, carrot cake is not my favorite cake; however, I do like it. Guess what Dad?"

"What?"

"How would you like me to mail you some carrot cupcakes?"

Surprised he replied, "Yes that would be great. You can do that?"

"Sure I can. I will send them after my fast that I am on and I will make them next week. I don't want to tempt myself by making the carrot cupcakes now because I will be too weak."

My father was overwhelmed. He could not believe his ears. He was finally going to get some carrot cake. Then he said, "Well, I can't wait."

The following Wednesday after Easter, I began to prepare dinner and the carrot cupcakes. I packed up eighteen cupcakes. I made the icing and packed it separately. I mailed the cupcakes the same day. A couple of days later, my father received his package.

My father was extremely excited. He said, "I got the cupcakes and this is the best carrot cake that I ever ate in my life. Thank you so much Daughter."

"You are welcomed Dad. You said that it is the best carrot cake you ever had in your life?"

"Yes, and my wife said she loved them too. They are great. However, I am trying to figure out how to get the one she ate back."

My father was making me laugh again and I was more happy that he was content. I replied, "I am glad you enjoyed them Dad, but it will be hard getting a cupcake out of your wife's stomach."

"I know, but I am not going to let her have any more. I am going to eat the rest of them by myself."

All I could say was, "Wow."

A few days later, my father called me. He was still stuck on those cupcakes. He could not quit talking about them. My father was in his second childhood. Excitement filled his environment. He became a different person. Dad normally does not ask me for anything but now his character had taken a turn where he swallowed his pride. The Bible says:

"Ye lust, and have not: ye kill, and desire to have, and cannot obtain: ye fight and war, yet ye have not, because ye ask not."
James 4:2 KJV

Boldly my father asked, "Daughter, can you make me some of those cupcakes for my birthday next month?"

Honored, I said, "Sure Dad. I will do that for you."

Taking a deep breath, he replied, "I don't think you know what I mean, you see, I want eighty-two cupcakes."

Totally floored I shouted, "Eighty-two cupcakes?"

Sternly he confirmed, "Yes eighty-two cupcakes; I want one for every year that I lived since I was born. I don't want one less or one more; I just want eighty-two cupcakes."

Since I did not have a job, I responded, "Dad, I can't afford the ingredients or the shipping fees for eighty-two cupcakes. I can only send you what I can afford."

Not taking no for an answer, he countered, "Daughter, I want eighty-two cupcakes for my birthday. This is what you do. Tell my grandson that he needs to pay for the ingredients and pay for the shipping fees. You cook and pack the cupcakes. This is what I want for my birthday. I have to have eighty-two cupcakes."

Considering that my father is my only living parent, I had to make sure his request happened. He humbled himself enough to ask not only me, but he also asked my son to grant him this birthday wish.

I surrendered and stated, "Okay Dad, I will talk to Bob J and see what he says."

"Thanks, I can't wait. Now, will you be sending them before my birthday or on my birthday? I don't want them after my birthday."

"Dad, they will be there before your birthday."

Excited he said, "Thanks and I will be calling to remind you. Next month seems like eternity. I want my cupcakes now. Oh and don't change the recipe. I want everything exactly like it was."

"No problem Dad, I will hook you up with the same cupcakes."

When we got off the phone, I was stunned that my father gave me this unusual request. I had to make it happen. I communicated my father's message to Bob J. My son just smiled. When we went to get groceries, he bought the ingredients for the cupcakes. My father and I talked almost every day. Our conversations would always be about the eighty-two cupcakes. He never let me off the phone until I would assure him that I was going to mail him his birthday present. He had another request that was just as big as the cupcakes.

My father called and asked, "Hey Daughter, I wanted to ask you something."

"What do you want to ask me Dad?"

What else could my father want as I pondered this in my mind?

"Well, what are the chances of you finishing 'I Hate God' on my birthday?"

I was pretty close to finishing this book. I would just have to push myself harder to make his request happen. I answered, "Dad I will do my best. I will make every effort possible to get the book finished for your birthday."

"That would be great Daughter. Do the best that you can. I would really love for the book to be released on my birthday if you can do it."

"I will do my best Dad."

In my spirit, I knew that I had to follow through with the desires that my father asked of me. The week before my father's birthday became very hectic. Unfortunately, I could not release this book on my father's birthday. May 24, 2015 was drawing nigh. There was too much work left and I could not honor his request. The Wednesday before his big day, I made his eighty-two carrot cupcakes and prepared them for shipment. While I was still making the cupcakes, I called my father.

Eager I said, "Dad I have the last batch of cupcakes in the oven."

My father responded, "I am really happy now. I will be excited for the rest of the day. When will they get here?"

I assured him and replied, "I am trying to get the cupcakes to you tomorrow.

"Wow, I am very excited. I can't wait, but I was lying about you making me eighty-two cupcakes."

While my father and I was laughing, I said, "Dad after what I have been through to make these cupcakes today, if I have to stuff them down your throat, you are going to eat all of these eighty-two cupcakes."

As my father was laughing, he said, "Oh you won't have to stuff them down my throat, because I just wanted to see what you would say Daughter."

Chuckling, I answered, "Well now you know."

We laughed and my father said something that really touched me. I could tell my father felt different about life itself and God when he said, "Daughter, when I get my cupcakes you are going to have to write another book about me."

"What book is that Dad?"

"When I get those cupcakes and start enjoying them, I want you to write another book about me and call it, I Love God."

Wow, I could not believe my ears. This was so different from meeting him in prison in 1976. I can only give God the glory for such a dynamic change and miracle. We got off the phone and I finished making the eighty-two cupcakes. I packed them and later on that afternoon, I mailed them overnight. The cupcakes made it to Iowa by noon the next day. To this day, my mind often ponders that my father wanted me to write another book about him and call it, 'I Love God.'

I HATE GOD

You hate God,
Someone told me,
I denied it,
Because it couldn't be.

I did not know,
What the Word said,
To love one master,
And hate the other instead.

My life was so full,
Of sin indeed,
I would not serve God,
Even in my need.

It did not matter,
If I died or not,
Sin felt good,
And Christ I forgot.

I backslid,
And wouldn't live right,
I would cuss all day,
And party all night.

I was told hate,
Is a strong word,
I refuse to believe,
Everything I heard.

I Hate God

Matthew 6:24,
Was all in my face,
It quicken my spirit,
Putting me in my place.

It said what I needed,
Whether I liked it or not,
If I did not listen,
My soul would rot.

I could not accept,
I hated God,
But that was the truth,
And I was a fraud.

My sins showed the world,
And showed me too,
That Satan was loved,
Instead of the God I knew.

This turned me around,
Cause this made me sick,
Repent to the Lord,
And do it real quick.

Forgive me God,
For hating You so,
Now I serve You Lord,
It's You I love You know.

He forgave me,
I won't look back,
I plead you now,
To get on the same track.

You don't need to live,
A life full of sin,
He is right there,
To receive you in.

He will forgive you,
No matter what you've done,
You were created to serve,
Your God the only One.

"It is finished."
John 19:30 KJV

Crisalyn B. Sachi is an author, minister, and a woman of God. Her inspiration comes from the Lord whom she serves. God gave her the gift of writing to help and encourage His people. Many people are lost and depressed. Coming from a time in her life of deep depression, Crisalyn ministers to those who need her. No one needs to live depressed in the midst of his or her sorrows. Crisalyn wrote 'I Hate God' out of obedience to God. The writing in this book is to stimulate a stronger walk with God. It is to motivate a life of worshipping our Heavenly Father. The book also encourages us to serve God with all we have through some mind-boggling experiences from the author and her father. God created us to serve and worship Him. Crisalyn is very grateful to represent God with the testimonies that He has given her. The Glory belongs to God.

46354941R10096

Made in the USA
San Bernardino, CA
05 March 2017